LETTERS TO TERESA

Earnest Epistles to One Inclined Toward
the Roman Catholic Church

by Samuel Fisk

$1.95

BIBLICAL EVANGELISM PRESS
P. O. Box 157
Brownsburg, Indiana 46112

Copyright ©, 1973, by

BIBLICAL EVANGELISM

ISBN: 0-914012-14-2

Cover Design by Ron Sumner

Printed in the United States of America

CONTENTS

AUTHOR'S NOTE

What follows grew out of actual correspondence with one who attended and seriously contemplated going into the Roman Catholic Church. A different name, however, is employed to avoid personal reference. Some documentation and supplemental material has been added to the initial correspondence, but all is being brought to the attention of the original party.

All Scripture quotations are taken from official Roman Catholic editions of the Bible; those in the New Testament usually from the Confraternity edition of 1941 (St. Anthony Guild Press), occasionally from other Catholic editions, as noted.

INTRODUCTION

My introduction to the chapters in this book came through the monthly paper, THE BIBLICAL EVANGELIST. I confess that at first I was a bit apprehensive, wondering if anything new could be added to the mounting pile of books and pamphlets on ROMANISM. But after reading the first installment I was ready for that which followed.

Mr. Fisk has written an interesting and informative work. His careful research in the teachings of the Roman Catholic Church and his interpretation of the Scriptures supported by clear exegesis meets a great need in this present hour.

Satan operates successfully in the area of religion, his most recent advances having been made in a charismatic movement involving Roman Catholics and Protestants. Today we have a new breed known as "evangelical catholics." But this title is a forgery. There is no such person. Mr. Fisk shows clearly that Rome has not changed, nor will she ever. His chapter, *Peter, the Rock and the Keys*, is superb. Read this book and pass it on to others.

LEHMAN STRAUSS, Litt. D.
Philadelphia, Pennsylvania

1

The Legacy Of Jesus' Sacrifice!

Is Continual Offering for Sin Needed Today?

Dear Teresa:

I take your word for it that you are very sincere in wanting to join the Roman Catholic Church. To the degree of your sincerity I can only express my respect.

I also recognize that you see in the observance of the Mass an impressive ceremony and stately ritualism. There is, indeed, an awe and solemnity in that rite which has wide appeal. And you are right, there are so many well-meaning and apparently intelligent people who attend and who seem convinced that it is the thing to do.

But the main question is, **how does God regard the matter?** Is it in accord with His declared will? Does He feel honored by the Mass and does He accept it for what it professes to be?

You no doubt have learned by this time that the Mass is really intended to be an offering of the body and blood of Christ upon the altars of the Roman Catholic churches; they claim that it is a solemn renewal of the sacrifice of Calvary each time it is performed. It is understood to be their most important sacrament, wherein "a true oblation" for sin is made and offered to God. I will show you shortly from their own official sources that this is what they claim.

But you may ask, *What is wrong with that? Isn't that really something to be thankful for, and should we not place confidence in such a well-provided sacrifice? Why shouldn't we participate in Christ's offered body and blood?*

The answer to these questions is that God has shown that no such sacrifice is in any way being made today, that Christ's blood is not really being offered now at all. God has set it down, instead, that His blessed Son made a **complete** and **final** sacrifice for sin when He gave Himself up once for all upon the cross —an offering not to be repeated because there is no need at all to repeat it. In fact, in this light, the attempt to renew such a sacrifice can be shown to be both disobedience to God's stated will and a complete lack of confidence in what has already been finished.

Perhaps I should not shock you at this point, but because this is true, the Mass is really a direct insult to God; it comes close to blasphemy as your own Bible will show you. Now before you react indignantly to such a statement or recoil from further considering it, let me set forth the basis for saying all of this.

I am aware that some Church authorities will say that Christ died on the Cross only once, and that the Mass is a bit different. They may say that at the crucifixion Jesus died for one type of sin only, as for Adamic (inherited) sin, or that in His death He paid for the eternal but not the temporal punishment for sin. But as we will soon see, He died for *all* sin and took upon Himself *all* the punishments due for every kind of sin.

Let us now look at some clear statements from God's Holy Word, and I will take them all from the official Confraternity New Testament [St. Anthony Guild Press, 1941], translated by the highest Catholic scholars and carrying the "approbration" of the Church.

Offerings For Sin—One or Many?

We may begin with the New Testament book of Hebrews. A large portion of this book—in fact six chapters (from the fifth to the tenth inclusive)—sets forth most emphatically the truth in this area. The thrust of the whole argument is the contrast between the ministrations of the Old Testament priests, their daily and repeated offerings, and that of our great New Testament priest, Christ, whose one sacrificial act was a complete and final accomplishment. Actually, those Levitical offerings, one following upon another, were merely pictures or types of the one glorious work of Christ on the cross which was to fulfill them and bring them to an end. It all shows the superiority of Christ's one work and God's full satisfaction therewith. Read those chapters for yourself.

See how it is put, for example, in Hebrews 7:23, 24, 27: *"And the other priests indeed were numerous, . . . but he, because he continues forever, has an everlasting priesthood. . . . He does not need to offer sacrifices daily (as the other priests did), . . . for the sins of the people; for this latter he did once for all in offering up himself."* (Parenthesis in Confraternity version.) Again note the contrast: *"For Jesus has not entered into a Holies made with hands, . . . nor yet has he entered to offer himself often, . . . But as it is, once for all at the end of the ages, he has appeared for the destruction of sin by the sacrifice of himself"* (Hebrews 9:24-26). Once more there is contrast: *"And every priest indeed stands daily ministering, and often offering the same sacrifices, which can never take away sins; but Jesus, having offered one sacrifice for sins, has taken his seat forever at the right hand of God"* (Hebrews 10:11, 12).

Did you notice the "one," "once," and "once for all" in the texts cited? Still further verses put the emphasis on this not-to-be-repeated aspect of our Lord's sacrificial work. We read again of how *"Christ . . . entered once for all through the greater and more perfect tabernacle, . . . by virtue of his own blood . . . having obtained eternal redemption"* (Hebrews 9:11, 12). Then, *"And just as it is appointed unto men to die once,"* and you and I will die only once, *"so also was Christ offered once to take away the sins of many"* (Verses 27, 28). Note the past tense throughout, indicating a completed action.

You see, of course, that the principle laid down is that the very repetition of sacrifices demonstrates their insufficiency. For if one were wholly sufficient there would be no need for repeating it. To repeat the sacrifice of Christ, therefore, is to declare its insufficiency! What a reproach upon the work of our blessed Lord, wrought at such a cost.

And did you notice in this ninth chapter the results of Christ's once-for-all work as it applies to us? These are strong terms: "obtained eternal redemption" (Verse 12), "the destruction of sin" (Verse 26), and "take away sins" (Verse 28). That being what was achieved, we certainly have no need for further sacrifice.

Now believe it or not, my friend, in the tenth chapter of Hebrews we find it put even stronger. In verse 10 it says, *". . . we have been sanctified through the offering of the body of Jesus Christ once for all."* That is clear and that is definite. Then in the 14th verse we read, *"For by one offering he has perfected forever those who are sancitfied."* Again I call attention to its results for us, "perfected forever." What more could you want? You can't add to perfection. Finally, if that were not clear enough, there is added, *"And their sins and their iniquities I will remember no more. Now where there is forgiveness of these, there is no longer offering for sin"* (Verses 17, 18). Notice especially the last phrase, "there is no longer offering for sin." So God says, "No more offering for sin." Why the Mass then? Why priests making an oblation? Not to take God's word for it being done, **all done,** is to disbelieve God and to disobey Him!

It is no wonder, then, that in this same general section of Hebrews there is solemn warning against some who might be in position to "crucify again for themselves the Son of God and make him a mockery" (6:6). What a terrible thing to make a mockery of our blessed Lord! And God says, further, *"How much worse punishments do you think he deserves who has trodden under foot the Son of God, and has regarded as unclean the blood of the covenant through which he was sanctified, and has insulted the spirit of grace?"* (10:29). So now you see why I said the attempt to renew the sacrifice of Christ is an "insult" to God. He says so Himself. Don't participate in what God says is a "mockery" and an "insult."

So that you may not think that the book of Hebrews is the only place setting forth the wonderful truth of the finished work of Christ, I may cite what St. Peter says. He declares, *"Christ also died once for sins, the Just for the unjust, that he might bring us to God"* (I Peter 3:18). If His death "once" brings us to God, what further need have we? (See also Romans 6:10.)

It becomes plain from all of this that the whole purpose of Christ's advent was to fulfill and bring to an end repeated sacrifices for sin. The Catholic Church is attempting to perpetuate that which Christ came to abolish—she is endeavoring to continue that which He died to bring to an end.

9

The Catholic Church Speaks

Let us turn now and see if the official Roman position is in accord with this strong and repeated Scripture testimony. I said that I would show you from authentic Catholic sources that what I said the Mass is supposed to be is really what the Church claims for it. I would not want to misrepresent her position. Let us therefore look at her highest authorities who have spoken for her.

I have stacked up on my desk as I write a pile of eighteen volumes, all authored by committed Roman Catholics and published by Catholic publishing houses, each book carrying the *Imprimatur* of some prominent dignitary in the hierarchy and a *Nihil Obstat* of some official in position to speak.[1] It would be interesting to quote from each one, but that would become very repetitious.

Many of these works cite the decrees of the Council of Trent, either referring to, quoting the decree, or giving the session involved and the numbers of the canons as references. Since Trent is the very highest authority and so widely recognized—giving the very edicts of the Church—let us see what it says about the matter of the Mass as an actual sacrifice.

First, I have the well-known *A Catholic Dictionary* by Addis, Arnold and Scannel, revised Seventeenth Edition. Under the article "Eucharist," it says, "The worship of sacrifice was not to cease in the Church, and the Council of Trent defines that in the Eucharist or Mass a true and proper sacrifice is offered to God. (Sess. xxii. can.1.)" Again, "On the cross and altar we have the same Victim and the same Priest, and therefore, in the words of the Council of Trent, the sacrifice of the Mass . . . is truly 'propitiatory.' (Sess. xxii, can. 3)" (pp. 321, 323).

A similar, more recent work is *A Catholic Dictionary (The Catholic Encyclopedic Dictionary)*, edited by D. Attwater, second edition, revised. Under "Sacrifice Of The Mass," we read, "The true sacrifice of the Body and Blood of Christ made present on the altar by the words of consecration; a repetition and a renewal of the offering made on Calvary; 'in this divine sacrifice the same Christ is present and immolated in a bloodless manner . . .' (Trent, Sess. xxii, can. 2)" (p. 443).

Now we might turn to the *Catechism of the Council of Trent*. My copy is the commonly used English one, translated and edited by McHugh and Callan, ninth printing, which I purchased in the Catholic Book Store in Manila, Philippines. It goes even further, saying, "The Eucharist was instituted by Christ . . . that the Church might have a perpetual Sacrifice, by which our sins might be expiated, and our heavenly Father, oftentimes grievously offended by our crimes, might be turned away from wrath to mercy." Again, "With regard to the institution of this Sacrifice,

---

1 *These terms stand for official approval by the Church.* "Nihil Obstat," *literally: nothing stands in the way, or nothing against it, so certified by a duly appointed censor.* "Imprimatur," *meaning: let it be printed, final approval, usually by a Bishop.*

the holy Council of Trent (Sess. xxii. cap. 1. canons 1, 2) . . . condemns under anathema all those who assert that in it is not offered to God a true and proper Sacrifice." Once more, "It must be taught without any hesitation that, as the holy Council (of Trent, Sess. xxii, cap. 2. canon; 3) has also explained, the sacred and holy Sacrifice of the Mass is not a Sacrifice of praise and thanksgiving only, or a mere commemoration of the Sacrifice performed on the cross, but also truly a propitiatory Sacrifice, by which God is appeased and rendered propitious to us. If, therefore, . . . we immolate and offer this most holy victim, we shall, without doubt, obtain mercy from the Lord" (pp. 255, 256, 258-259).

Another similar work which has gone through many editions is *The Catechism Explained* by F. Spirago, edited by R. F. Clarke. In it are the statements: "The Mass is consequently no mere image of the sacrifice of the cross; it is not a bare memorial of it, it is the selfsame sacrifice which was consumated on Calvary (Council of Trent, 22, 3), and accordingly it is of the selfsame value and of the selfsame efficacy. . . . The oblation once offered upon the cross is renewed upon the altar." And, "To make atonement is preeminently the object of the sacrifice of the Mass; this is the chief intention for which it is celebrated" (pp. 541, 542, 547).

But why go on? I have two books dealing with the well-known "Baltimore Catechism." One is *An Explanation of the Baltimore Catechism* by T. L. Kinkead. (It contains two Imprimatures and two Nihil Obstats, and, further, six full pages of Approbations by eminent Catholic dignitaries.) Questions 265 and 266 are answered in very much the same way as what I have already cited. So is the case also with *The Baltimore Catechism No. 3, With Explanations,* by E. M. Deck, fourth edition, under questions 321, 323, 324, etc. Of course, all of these works try to make the Mass seem rational, and there is a pretense to be scriptural, but as you can see for yourself, they do absolute violence to the revealed truth of Holy Writ which I have called to your attention.

Why, oh why, invent such a humanly devised system? Why, oh why, run so completely contrary to what we have seen God clearly declares? The plain testimony of Holy Scriptures is so far different from these elaborate and cunningly reasoned schemes. How much simpler just to place faith in Christ's one work, as we have seen, completely finished upon the cross.

And how much more noble a view of God and His matchless grace, to see Him having made all the provision, and full provision, for all man's needs. In fact, for any man to undertake to engage in any part of making a sacrifice for sin removes it entirely from the grace of God. See Romans 11:6; 4:4.

In view of what we have seen that the Catholic New Testament itself sets forth, the statements of dogma cited are quite shocking. They are an affront to intelligence and common reason, violate good taste, and run counter to man's sense of objective facts. All this—*in addition to contradicting outright the clear Word of God.*

Still more shocking are some further statements which show what is regarded as involved in the dogma of the Mass. Certain

11

declarations from highly regarded sources are almost unbelievable. For example, in a book entitled *The Mass,* by P. C. Yorke, third edition, no less than Cardinal Manning is quoted (from his *Eternal Priesthood,* chap. 2) as saying, "He perpetuates His humility in the Blessed Sacrament, and places Himself in the hands of His creatures, and is bid, morning by morning, by their word to be present upon the altar; and is by them lifted up, and carried to and fro, and, in the end, He is received by the worthy and by the unworthy" (p. 56).

In another book, *A Manual of Theology For the Laity,* by P. Geiermann (Imprimatur, Archbishop John M. Farley), I read, "Jesus Christ . . . daily offers Himself for the same purpose on the altar as He did on Calvary. . . . Jesus Christ uses the agency of His duly ordained minister at the altar, even as He used the blind agency of the executioners on Calvary" (p 370). I will spare you the comment I might make.

Some refer to the Mass as "an unbloody offering of the body and blood of Christ." To many that appears as a wholly inconsistent contradiction of terms. Yet some of the most highly placed authorities refer to the Mass as a shedding of Christ's blood. Even Cardinal Gibbons so states in his famous book, *The Faith of Our Fathers* (one hundred and tenth edition). He says, "Let us represent to ourselves the Mass as another Calvary, which it is in reality. . . . If the wounds of the Martyrs plead so elequently for us, how much more eloquent is the blood of Jesus shed daily upon our altars?" (pp. 260, 261).

In a more recent work, *The Faith Of Millions,* by John A. O'Brien of Notre Dame, we find exactly the same words in the last sentence above as being this scholarly writer's view also (p. 359). Then O'Brien further says, "When the priest pronounces the tremendous words of consecration, he reaches up into the heavens, brings Christ down from His throne, and places Him upon our altar to be offered up again as the victim for the sins of man. . . . The priest brings Christ down from Heaven, and renders Him present on our altar as the eternal Victim for the sins of man—not once but a thousand times! The priest speaks and lo! Christ, the eternal and omnipotent God, bows his head in humble obedience to the priest's command" (p. 268).

I will bring to your attention another, if it will not repel your more delicate sensibilities. In a very modern work, with an appeal to the up-to-date mind, it appears without apology. *The Faith Explained,* by Leo J. Trese, says in connection with our main topic, "If a person should happen to be struck by an unexpected attack of nausea after receiving Holy Communion and should vomit the Sacred Host—then the Sacred Host should be gathered up in a clean linen cloth and given to the priest for disposal. If the priest is not available, or it is doubtful whether the appearance of bread still remain—then the stomach-contents should be enclosed in a linen cloth and burned" (p. 428).

The question may occur here, *Have not some of these things changed? What is the situation now in the light of Vatican II?*

By way of answer we may go to the official pronouncements

of that Council. The same essential dogmas are still embraced.

For example, we read, "At the Last Supper, on the night when He was betrayed, our Saviour instituted the eucharistic sacrifice of His Body and Blood. He did this in order to perpetuate the sacrifice of the Cross throughout the centuries. . . . a paschal banquet in which Christ is eaten." And, "by offering the Immaculate Victim . . . through the hands of the priest. . . ." (*The Sixteen Documents of Vatican II*, Daughters of St. Paul edition, pp. 31, 32).

In another place we find these words: "As often as the sacrifice of the cross in which Christ our Passover was sacrificed is celebrated on the altar, the work of our redemption is carried on" (Ibid., p. 111).

Again, "Taking part in the eucharistic sacrifice, which is the fount and apex of the whole Christian life, they offer the Divine Victim to God. . . ." (Ibid., p. 120).

Finally, "The Lord left behind . . . that sacrament of faith where natural elements refined by man are changed into His glorified Body and Blood" (Ibid., p. 549).

These excerpts are taken from different, but representative, documents of the Council. So you see, little has changed.

All Sin Covered At Calvary

Now, dear friend, it may be that someone will say that the one work of Christ which we have emphasized covers only certain sins (as orignal sin, or inherited sin), or only one phase of sin (as eternal versus temporal punishments). But in the Holy Scripture we do not find these or any other such distinctions in different types of sin. But we do find the promise of God is that all sin—**absolutely all sin**—was met and paid for by that one perfect work of Christ on the cross.

To show you that this is so, let me quote again from your Confraternity New Testament (and I will put in capital letters the word **all** to emphasize that all sin is included):

In the First Epistle of John, chapter one, we read the simple statement, *"The blood of Jesus Christ, his Son, cleanses us from ALL sin"* (Verse 7). Again, *"He is faithful and just to forgive us our sins and to cleanse us from ALL iniquity"* (Verse 9).

In Titus 2:13, 14, we read the wonderful statement, *"Our great God and Savior, Jesus Christ, who gave himself for us that he might redeem us from ALL iniquity and cleanse for himself an acceptable people."*

Colossians 2:13, 14, says, *"And you, when you were dead by reason of your sins . . . he brought to life along with him, forgiving you ALL your sins, cancelling the decree against us, which was hostile to us. Indeed, he has taken it completely away, nailing it to the cross."* I like that added phrase, "taken it completely away." You see how full and comprehensive His great work on the cross for us was.

One more citation will suffice, and any one of these should settle the matter. In Acts 13:38, 39, we read the statement, *"Be it known therefore to you, brethren, that through him forgiveness of sins is proclaimed to you, and in him everyone who believes is acquitted of ALL the things of which you could not be acquitted by the Law of Moses."*

These are wonderful promises and they leave no question of God's one full provision for our salvation. Did you notice in the last reference the single condition of that salvation? It is freely offered to "everyone who believes." Again, in just a couple of chapters earlier (Acts 10:43), it says, *"To him all the prophets bear witness, that through his name all who believe in him may receive forgiveness of sins."* So there it is again. Only to truly "believe" is to receive forgiveness of sins.

Won't you, dear friend, do what God says and accept it **all** just by faith? Humbly call upon Christ, telling Him that you accept that one perfect atonement for all your sins. Then you will become a child of God and be saved forever. Then Christ will keep you and continually save you from sin without further sacrifice. Read the seventh chapter of Hebrews, which makes this so clear. Rituals and priestly functions avail nothing. Cast yourself on Christ alone. He will give you the assurance that you are His and that you have everlasting life. Oh, take it— *take it now!*

2

Does One Receive Christ Literally in the Sacrament?

How Is Christ's Offering for Sin to be Partaken?

Dear Teresa:

I am glad that you are giving serious consideration to what I have brought to your attention. I appreciate your saying that I have made some things clear and that you can follow the line of thought presented. Intelligent and well educated as you are, you should be able to see the reasoning behind these things. But you are still wavering. Let us, therefore, look at some other aspects of the subject.

Teresa, you have observed the great reverance which Catholics show upon entering their churches and especially upon passing the central point of one. They genuflect or go down on one knee; they bow and cross themselves; on certain days they will go down the aisle toward the altar on their knees, repeating prayers or saying the rosary as they proceed. But do you know why they display such reverence toward the front of the sanctuary? It is because they believe that Deity, in the person of Christ, is actually present upon their altars. You see, after the consecration of the host, they believe that the wafer is really Christ Himself. At communion, all the elements are not consumed; some is always left to be kept deposited on the altar as an object of worship. It is placed under a special elaborate covering or in a particular container, and it is the focal point of the whole church the most sacred spot in the entire edifice.

Of course, there is nothing in Holy Scripture to suggest anything like all this; it is man-devised and a purely human addition to what God has laid down. To that extent it is complete disobedience to God because He has said that He "does not dwell in temples built by hands; neither is he served by human hands" (Acts 17:24, 25; also 7:48), and, "We have . . . in the heavens . . . the true tabernacle, which the Lord has erected and not man" (Hebrews 8:1, 2), and "Be ye . . . built into a spiritual house . . . to offer spiritual sacrifices" (I Peter 2:5). Therefore we are told to "Mind the things that are above, not the things that are on earth" (Colossians 3:2).

Jesus' Words, "This Is My Body," Examined

As to Christ being literally present on Church altars, the question arises, what about Jesus' words of consecration when

He instituted the sacrament? Didn't He say, "This is my body"? Yes; and the words are often repeated with emphasis on the "is,"—"This *is* my body." That would seem to indicate that it is His real body which is at issue.

However, several reasons show clearly that Jesus did not intend these words to be taken literally. Let us honestly face them and I am sure you will see it for yourself. I present two major and several minor considerations.

First of all, the idea of the bread and wine becoming the actual body and blood of Jesus by His words of so-called consecration is directly contradicted by the further words of Jesus on that occasion. Notice in Matthew 26, where Jesus spoke the words which the Church insists made the elements true flesh and blood, Jesus *afterward* referred to that which they were receiving as "this fruit of the vine" (Verse 29, Confraternity). Accordingly, it was fruit of the vine and not blood, at this subsequent time. His saying "this fruit of the vine" shows that it referred to the very element which He held in His hand and over which He had made His pronouncement, it then not being anything different.

Similarly, in the record of the institution in I Corinthians 11, *after* the words of "consecration" were spoken (Verses 24, 25), Jesus is quoted as speaking of the element as "bread," in verse 26, "as often as ye shall eat of this bread" (quite evidently looking forward to frequent observances), it being on each occasion just "bread." Again, in verse 28, "so let him eat of that bread." Thus the idea of transubstantiation[1] breaks down completely.

Our second main thought here is that we see beyond question that figures of speech were employed on this occasion. In fact, a double figure.

In instituting the supper Jesus said, "This cup . . . drink it" (I Corinthians 11:25); and, "drink the cup" (Verse 26); and, "whoever . . . drinks the cup" (Verse 27). Now, of course, no one thinks that they were told to swallow a literal, material cup. Jesus certainly used the term "cup" as a figure—metonymy, the container standing for the thing contained.

Going on, Jesus says, "This cup is the new covenant in my blood" (Verse 25), and the same in Luke (22:20), "This cup is the new covenant." Now did the disciples drink a literal covenant or that which stood for or was a sign and seal of a covenant? To ask the question is to answer it. This is a metaphor. So here we have two clear types of figures of speech. All this establishes beyond question Jesus' principle of using symbolic language.

In Jesus' discourse on the same occasion, in the upper room, we find Him speaking of being "the vine" and of our being "the branches" (John 15:5), words obviously figurative. Yet just as He said, "This *is* my body," so He said, "I *am* the vine." Why press the literalness of one more than the other? The people of the

---

[1] *Transubstantiation* is defined as follows in *A Catholic Dictionary* by Adis, Arnold, *et al* (seventeenth edition): "It is not enough to confess Christ's Real Presence in the Eucharist. The Council of Trent requires us further to confess the 'change of the whole substance of the bread into the Body, of the whole substance of the wine into the Blood [of Christ], only the appearance of bread and wine remaining; which change the Catholic Church most fitly calls transubstantiation.' " (Brackets in original.)

East who heard Him speak loved figures of speech, frequently employed them, and readily understood their use. Indeed, elsewhere in the passion week just preceding the last supper, Jesus spoke in figures (Matthew 23:24, "swallow the camel"; 33, "ye serpents") and in parables (Matthew 24:32, 33; 25:1f., 14f., 33).

When Jesus therefore said, "This is my body," He quite evidently meant, "This represents or symbolizes my body given in death for your sins." In fact, His saying, "This do in remembrance of me" (I Corinthians 11:24, 26), shows that it was just that—in remembrance—and not as an actual source of redemption or means of effecting divine grace.

To take the words literally further involves us in several problems, if not utter inconsistencies or well-nigh absurdities. Let us look at some of them.

First, Jesus stood there (or reclined) in His literal body, a complete body. If He held in His hands that which also was His body, He must have had two bodies.

Secondly, and even the suggestion of this is shocking, did they all eat of His actual body? That is quite a reprehensible thought, even implying (dare I say it?) something akin to cannibalism.

Thirdly, the Church tells us that Jesus' disciples on that occasion ate that body as a true sacrifice and sacrament. But it was not yet broken on the cross, not yet offered for the sin of the world. Then we are told that it was a sacrifice before the great sacrifice, just as the passover was. However, observing the passover was a memorial or a type, and no one ever said that the passover lamb became something else when offered. Just so, no one ever said that the bread and cup were more than a symbol and a memorial.

Fourthly, when the literal meaning of the words, "This is my body," are insisted upon, we might ask a simple question. Jesus stood before His disciples in His living body; He held in His hands that over which He spoke the words. If, then, "This is my body," meant His literal flesh, was that which He held His living body or His dead body? It must be replied, His dead body, for He said, "my body which is broken for you." Did He then have a living body and a dead body at the same time?

Fifthly, while we believe in the spiritual omnipresence of our Lord, yet we never read of His human body being in more than one place at a time, and Scripture indicates that His actual body is now present only at the right hand of the Father (Hebrews 1:3; 10:12; 12:2; Acts 2:33; 3:21; Colossians 3:1). Furthermore, it distinctly says, *"Do not say in thy heart: Who shall ascend into heaven? (that is, to bring down Christ),"* [parenthesis in Confraternity], and, *"Even though we have known Christ according to the flesh, yet now we know him so no longer"* (Romans 10:6; II Corinthians 5:16).

Sixth, the miracles of Christ and the apostles were always characterized by being evident to the natural human senses—the witness of sight, smell, touch and taste always confirmed them. This is not the case in respect to the "miracle" of the bread and wine becoming the actual body and blood of Christ. Everyone who partakes is conscious that the elements feel and taste far different from literal flesh. Therefore, no such miracle as is claimed takes place in the eucharist.

In view of all this, let us take the reasonable and the scriptural position on the matter and rest the case there.

What Does "Eat the Flesh of the Son of Man" Mean?

Let me say, my friend, that I have checked many Catholic sources: Catholic encyclopedias, Catholic dictionaries, Catholic catechisms and instruction books, etc. I have been surprised to find over and over again that these Catholic authorities appeal for justifying their practice to the sixth chapter of St. John's Gospel. They quote certain statements which taken alone seem to be strong grounds for what they claim. But they very conveniently leave out parts of the passage which show just the opposite. They refer only to these verses (and again I quote from the Confraternity version): *"Jesus therefore said to them, 'Amen, Amen, I say to you, unless you eat the flesh of the Son of Man, and drink his blood, you shall not have life in you. He who eats my flesh and drinks my blood has life everlasting. . . . He who eats my flesh and drinks my blood, abides in me and I in him.'"* (Verses 54-57 in Confraternity; 53-56, K.J.V.)

Yet other statements of Jesus, right in this connection, show that He did not—**and could not**—have meant this literally. Let me show you five or six things which indicate what Jesus did mean, and that it was not the continual offering in the Mass which He had in mind.

First, and this alone should settle it, in verse 64 (63, K.J.V.) Jesus reached the focal point of His remarks by saying, *"It is the spirit that gives life; the flesh profits nothing. The words that I have spoken to you are spirit and life."* So Jesus distinctly said that it is the spirit, and *not* the flesh, which is the vital thing that He had in mind. The Church says that it must be regarded as Jesus' actual flesh to fulfill it, but Jesus Himself said "the flesh profits nothing," but that "the spirit gives life." And then He put the emphasis on His Words, and therefore we should feed our souls on His Word, that is, the Holy Scriptures.

The Jews to whom Jesus spoke the words could not see that He meant it literally. They asked, "How can this man give us his flesh to eat?" (Verse 53; 52, K.J.V.). The reason they doubted it was that to a faithful Jew the eating of blood, or of flesh with the blood in it, was exceedingly abhorant, and it was forbidden by their law (Leviticus 3:17; 7:26; 17:14; Acts 15:20, 29). And remember, these around Him, as well as the first believers, were all Jews. Surely they would not have abandoned their deeply ingrained convictions without a struggle, without some very clear, positive and detailed instructions to do so. But of such we find none.

Second, in verse 59 (58, K.J.V.), Jesus said, *"This is the bread that has come down from heaven; not as your fathers ate the manna, and died."* In other words, it was not an actual eating such as was the case with the children of Israel when they ate the manna in the wilderness; it is not literal bread of which someone can partake as of food. The children of Israel received the manna in their mouths and swallowed it. That is just what Jesus said He did not have in mind. So here again it is a spiritual partaking, a feeding of the soul, to which He had reference.

Third, in this same connection—in fact, in leading up to the verses under consideration—Jesus said, *"Amen, amen, I say unto you, he who believes in me has life everlasting"* (Verse 47). This is a clear, positive declaration. It is unqualified, and it shows all that is necessary to receive "life everlasting." Its significance here is that it indicates the real import of this discussion, that of "eating the flesh of the Son of Man." It gives the key to Jesus' meaning. Since, then, the one who "believes" on Him "has life everlasting," nothing more is required, and what follows must obviously be illustrative of this. To turn around and insist that something else quite different is essential to salvation would be entirely inconsistent, and Jesus never contradicts Himself.

Fourth, look now at the fortieth verse. It is in the heart of Jesus' discourse about "eating" His flesh. He says, "whoever beholds the Son, and believes. . . ." If we take things strictly in the literal sense then we must actually see or "behold" Jesus to have everlasting life. How many, now, have really seen Jesus? I have heard of some notable saints who claim to have actually seen the Virgin Mary, but I do not recall any lately who have said that they saw Jesus. Then none comply with the words and none has everlasting life. You say this is ridiculous; but why press some of Jesus' words in the literal sense and not others in the same connection? Here, surely is inconsistency. Obviously, to "behold" the Son is to see Him by faith, just as to "eat the flesh" is to partake by faith.

Fifth, in verse 58 (57, K.J.V.), Jesus shows just how one is to "eat" Him. He says, *"As the living Father has sent me, and as I live because of the Father, so he who eats me, he also shall live because of me."* Note the "as" and the counterpart "so." The one gives the measure of the other. And what is the standard? Jesus says it is "as I live because of the Father." In the manner by which He lives because of the Father, in like manner we are to live by Him. His life in the Father was one of spiritual association, not one of any material participation. There was no literally embracing of anything to give Him life in the Father. In the very same way, He says, we are to "eat" Him by a spiritual involvement. And that is all. Jesus Himself gave the true explanation. Let us not press it beyond that.

Sixth, and this has been so easily overlooked, three times Jesus distinctly said that you must, if you take it literally, "eat the flesh of the Son of Man, AND drink his blood," otherwise "you shall not have life in you" (Verse 54; 53, K.J.V.). Again, "He who eats my flesh AND drinks my blood has life everlasting. . . . He who eats my flesh, AND drinks my blood, abides in me and I in him" (Verses 55, 57; 54, 56, K.J.V., emphasis mine). Now you know that the cup has long been withheld from all but the priests. In other words, people partook in one kind only; that is, they received the wafer alone, or that which after consecration was supposed to be the very body of Christ. But they never received the cup or that which is supposed to be the blood of Christ. Thus, by the very passage appealed to, they actually have no life in them, for they do not drink of that which Jesus appeared to say they must drink .

Now Catholic authorities have been hard pressed to justify this.[2] Therefore they had to resort to the strategem of decreeing that any particle of the consecrated wafer contains Christ "whole and entire," and that the communicant thereby receives the benefit of all. Of course there is no direct statement in Scripture to this effect. But if Christ is received whole and entire under either form, why did He institute both, and command through the Apostle Paul that those in the church, as at Corinth, should "eat" of the bread AND "drink" of the cup (I Corinthians 10:16; 11:28)? But good Catholics for years have not partaken of both, which, by their own interpretation, would deprive them of everlasting life.

Even if by receiving the bread—flesh (?)—they therein receive the blood, still they do not "drink" it. If the passage is to be taken strictly and literally, they should "drink," which you and I know they have not done.

Incidentally, if by receiving communion in one kind the communicant receives the benefit of it all, or receives it "mystically," why not extend it just a little more and say that by receiving the elements as representative or as symbolical of Christ, one fulfills the basic requirements? That would be just as reasonable, and in fact more in harmony with Scripture taken as a whole.

Therefore, the John 6 passage, quite obviously, is a picture, a figure or illustration of what Christ meant. It is the same as where, two chapters preceding, He said at the well of Sychar, *"Everyone who drinks of this water will thirst again. He, however, who drinks of the water that I shall give him shall never thirst; but the water that I will give him shall become in him a fountain of water, springing up unto life everlasting"* (John 4:13, 14). No literal water is employed, nor is there anything that we are involved with that turns into something else when applied. Similarly, a bit further on, Jesus becomes to us the "door" (John 10:9) and we are the "sheep" (Verse 7). Thus the one, just as much as the others, is to be taken in a spiritual sense.

Jesus giving His flesh for the life of the world (John 6:52; 51, K.J.V.), quite obviously, then, refers to His giving His body in sacrifice for us upon the cross when He was crucified and suffered "in the flesh" (I Peter 3:18; 4:1). And our partaking of it is our accepting it for ourselves or putting our trust in that sacrificial death for sin. He meant that just *as* the body feeds on ordinary bread, *so* our soul may feed on Him by embracing His offering of Himself upon the cross, accepting it individually by truly claiming it as

2 The Council of Trent gives, among the reasons why the cup is withheld from the laity, the point that (after consecration) the species of the wine which remains for the adoration of the faithful or to be conveyed to the sick "might turn acid"! (Catechism of The Council of Trent, p. 252.) How that which, by supernatural miracle, is already transformed into the actual blood of the Savior could turn into "acid" is not explained. (True blood might mold or decay, but only wine could turn into acid.)

the sufficient atonement to cover and take away all of our guilt.

When transubstantiation is insisted upon, Catholic authorities tell us that in receiving the host (consecrated wafer) we must take by faith that it is the real and actual flesh of Christ. If taste or sense seem to indicate otherwise, let faith overcome the obstacles—accept it by faith that it is what the Church says it is. Here the appeal made really brings us closer to the truth we see in Scripture: **it is an act of faith that counts.** But if faith is so vital, if faith is the key, we can very readily go one step further and accept the truth that it is *faith* in Christ which is the essential factor; the eating and drinking in this case is an act of faith.

3

Priestly Powers Versus Blessings for All Believers

Did Jesus Invest Church Leaders With Unfailing Authority?

Dear Teresa:

You say that the points which I have made seem to have
something in their favor, but that there are other things which
should also be taken into account. Well, the Church has built
up an elaborate and complex system, and it would become very
involved to go into all the ramifications which might be touched
upon, even though you ask for detailed explanations. But by
just dealing with some of the major points I think that you
will see that the foundation of the whole is involved, and that
should take care of secondary things.

You reluctantly acknowledge that what I said is right if we
base everything on Holy Scripture, in which case the Church
has gone beyond what is warranted. But you question that Scripture alone is our authority. You have been given to understand
that Jesus provided that upon His authorized representatives on
earth would be bestowed unfailing divine wisdom to lead His
Church into further truth, truth of equal importance to that in Holy
Writ. This being so, they could declare all that is necessary
and decree matters about the holy sacraments which do not
depend upon what is found in the Bible.

Here I must admit that many of those who have undertaken
to discuss Romanism have overlooked this which is probably the
most basic concept underlying the Church's claims. There has
been wide failure to recognize that the average Catholic assumes
without further argument that his Church is right because it was
appointed to be custodian of the truth for all men and ordained
to be the channel of redemption, the channel whereby the means of
grace would be made available to the world. Much discussion, indeed,
would seem to have missed the mark if all that is necessary for
one to know is that a church not subject to error teaches a
certain thing and that the common person can just rest the case
there. So we need to go back and examine the first principle,
investigate the validity of this basic claim.

To begin with, if Jesus made such provision for a church
which is authoritarian in the person of its leaders, the only way
we would know of it is by what He said and directed as revealed

in the New Testament. Otherwise we would be arguing in a circle, saying that the church is a true authority because it says it is a true authority!

But the Church itself seems to belie such unquestioned authority because in all of its attempts to prove further matters it makes a desperate appeal to Scripture. If it was given absolute authority, it should really not matter whether or not its additional pronouncements can be found in Scripture. (Incidentally, that is just the position taken by the Mormon church.)

The most pivotal element in the Church's claim is that upon the apostles was bestowed a special enduement of the Holy Spirit, that He was peculiarly vouchsafed to them, and that therefore they and the Church which they were to direct would be shown all truth and would be kept from error. Actually, there is no proof at all that the apostles alone were endued with an exclusive bestowment of the Holy Spirit; in fact, just the opposite, as will be seen by examining Jesus' words of promise.

Look first at what the Church claims.

Cardinal Gibbons, in his famous book, *The Faith of Our Fathers*, says, "Jesus sends forth the Apostles with plenipotentiary powers to preach the Gospel. . . . The Apostles and their successors have received full powers to announce the gospel; and on the other [hand], their hearers are obliged to listen with docility and to obey. . . ." (p. 56). Then on the next page, as proof, the Cardinal quotes John 14:16 and 16:13, which we will consider in a moment.

The same texts are cited in O'Brien's popular *The Faith of Millions*, where that writer says, "Christ promises to send the Holy Ghost, the Spirit of truth, upon the Apostles" (p. 136).

In the *Catechism of The Council of Trent*, which I quoted earlier, we find a rather shocking statement: "The Spirit, first imparted to the Apostles, has by the infinite goodness of God always continued in the Church. And just as this one Church cannot err in faith or morals, since it is guided by the Holy Ghost; so, on the contrary, all other societies arrogating to themselves the name of *church*, must necessarily, because guided by the spirit of the devil, be sunk in the most pernicious errors, both doctrinal and moral" (p. 107).

Whether this guidance of the Holy Spirit was given only to the apostles and their official successors is the point we want to examine. To show that the Church emphatically asserts this, I quote from *Handbook of The Christian Religion* by W. Wilmers, S. J. and J. Conway, S. J. (Revised second edition; Imprimatur, Patric J. Hayes, Archbishop of New York). There we read, "The apostles, not the faithful, were directly invested by Christ with that power which He conferred on His Church. . . . The Catholic doctrine, contained in Holy Scripture, is, that Christ conferred His authority *immediately on the apostles,* to be exercised by them independently of the faithful; consequently, that the Church is, by divine institution, an unequal society, consisting of superiors and subjects. . . . The power intrusted to the Church has not been conferred on the body of the faithful. . . . The power promised was *conferred on the apostles alone*" (pp. 78, 79; emphasis in original).

Is that true?

23

Christ's Promise Of the Holy Spirit Examined

What is assumed to be the final ground for this broad claim is seen in the words of Jesus, so confidently asserted to be directed to His Apostles (as if to no others), as found in John 14:16, 17, and 16:13, 14. There, Jesus, soon to depart, gave the promise of the coming of the Holy Spirit. I quote (from the Confraternity version): *"And I will ask the Father, and he will give you another Advocate to dwell with you forever, the Spirit of truth whom the world cannot receive."* And, *"But when he, the Spirit of truth, has come, he will teach you all the truth . . . he will receive of what is mine and declare it to you."*

Several things need to be observed here. These words were part of Jesus' upper-room discourse on the night of His betrayal. The whole discourse of about three and a half chapters (from John 13:31 to 16:33) has been a source of deep instruction and inestimable blessing to all the people of God throughout the centuries. It contains the matchless promise of a place prepared in Heaven (14:1-6), the legacy of peace amid earthly trials (14:27; 15:11; 16:33), the assurance of our Lord's care and concern for His own (14:18; 15:15), promises to answer prayer (14:13, 14; 15:7; 16:24), and so on. Certainly all of this was not just for the leaders of the Church, but for **all** the children of God.

These chapters, indeed, contain exhortations for common believers, broad admonitions which all of us should take to heart. Read these chapters for yourself and you will see what I mean. Great loss has been entailed by not just taking the Bible and reading it as it is and accepting it for its own sake. In the midst of all of this general, widely applicable teaching are the promises of Jesus to send the Holy Spirit to abide with His true followers. How, in the full light of this wonderful passage, can anyone pick out certain statements and say that they are only for the apostles and their chosen successors?

While spoken to a certain group of disciples, it is quite evident that Jesus was reaching out beyond them to all of His true followers. He said, *"If anyone love me, he will keep my word . . ."* (14:23); *"He who has my commandments and keeps them . . ."* (14:21); and, *"He who abides in me . . . If anyone does not abide . . ."* (15:5, 6). The promises are to those—anyone—who love Him and keep His word. Do only the clergy love God and seek to please Him? You and I, certainly, should aim to love God and keep His commandments. Then the promises are to such as us.

There is no phrase in this entire upper-room discourse of our Lord employing the terms *apostles, the twelve,* or anything implying that only the leaders of the Church were included. On the contrary, in chapter 14:12, just a couple of verses preceding the one promising the Spirit, we find that Jesus said, "He who believes in me, . . ." and to such, great things are promised. Note that it is to those "who believe," not those who would take certain solemn vows and be consecrated by august ecclesiastics, or those who arriving through elaborately prescribed steps would assume to direct the church, or those who would devote themselves to a vocation in which they would live apart from the common people, but just to those—all of us—who would believe.

Similarly, the commission and promises following Jesus' resurrection, often assumed to be only for a restricted group, given likewise in the upper-room, were not given alone to the twelve apostles, or eleven (Judas having passed on). A very much overlooked statement in this connection is found in the parrallel account as presented by St. Luke. In the chapter recording these things in his gospel, we read that the Emmaus disciples on the resurrection day returned to Jerusalem "where they found the Eleven gathered together and those who were with them" (Luke 24:33). Note the words "and those who were with them." Accordingly, it was more than the eleven apostles. How many more we do not know. But these two from Emmaus easily joined them, as others quite evidently did, for they found a larger number already there.[1] Anyway, it was to this larger group that Jesus committed the gospel for the world. And a few days later, following the ascension, there were gathered in the upper room a mixed assembly of 120 persons (Acts 1:13-15) who apparently were those endowed with the Holy Spirit on the day of Pentecost.

That much neglected phrase "and those who were with them" may be seen in other places also. For example in Mark 4:10, where we read, "Those who were with him and the Twelve asked him about the parables." Therefore the group of Apostles may not have been such an exclusive club as has sometimes been assumed.

The verses which we noted in John 14 and 16 speak of being led into all truth and being shown the things of Christ. This no doubt included a guarantee of the accuracy of the New Testament which some of them would help to compose. Not all the New Testament was written by Apostles. Some others who were not Apostles (nor their official successors) were used to record the Holy Scriptures, as for example, St. Mark. St. Luke, too, was not one of the Apostles, neither of the original twelve nor later referred to in Scripture as an apostle. Yet he, like Mark, was certainly led into the truth, and through such as them the things done and spoken by the Lord were infallibly recorded.

There is nothing to show that the fulness of the Spirit was given to the officers of the church alone. Quite otherwise. Scripture not only makes clear that all believers have the Holy Spirit,[2] but also that all can be "filled" with the Spirit (Acts 4:31; 13:52; Ephesians 5:18), and be "led" by the Spirit (Romans 8:14; Galatians 5:18).

In writing to the believers in Ephesus, those who had "faith in the Lord Jesus" (Ephesians 1:15, 16), the Apostle Paul prays *"that the God of our Lord Jesus Christ, the Father of glory,*

---

[1] Of four Roman Catholic commentaries on the Gospels which I have, only one refers in any way to this passage in Luke. In *The Word of Salvation, A Commentary on The Gospels,* by the Jesuite scholars Valensin, Huby, & Durand, (translated by J. J. Heenan) we read: "The Apostles gathered in company with other disciples. . . . The Apostles were not alone; they were surrounded by other disciples" (Vol. II, p. 431).

[2] John 7:37-39; Acts 5:32; 13:52; Romans 5:5; 8:9; I Corinthians 3:16; 6:19; 12:3, 13; Galatians 4:6; Titus 3:5, 6; I John 4:13.

may grant you the spirit of wisdom and revelation in deep knowledge of him: the eyes of your mind being enlightened, so that you may know what is the hope of his calling, . . . and what the exceeding greatness of his power towards us who believe" (Ephesians 1:17-19). Note the last phrase; it is for those "who believe." That includes all of us. And the thrust of it is that we common believers may have "the spirit of wisdom and revelation in deep knowledge," and that we can be "enlightened." In chapter 3:16-19 of the same book, the apostle similarly expresses the desire that the Lord would strengthen the believers "with power through his Spirit" so that they would be able to "comprehend" and "be filled unto all the fulness of God." None should dare to arrogate such privileges to a select few.

One more passage with the same thrust. St. John writes in later years to the believers of his day, to those whom in I John 2 he calls "my dear children" (Verses 1, 12, 18, 28). This was for all believers generally. Now see what he says in verses 20 and 27: *"But you have an anointing from the Holy One and you know all things. . . . As for you, let the anointing which you have received from him, dwell in you, and you have no need that anyone teach you. But as his anointing teaches you concerning all things, and is true and is no lie, even as it has taught you, abide in him."* Here we see three things: 1. More than just some selected clergy have the anointing from "the Holy One." 2. That anointing instructs us, as we abide in Him (27,c), concerning all things. 3. We therefore "have no need that anyone teach" us!

That completely sweeps away the idea of any limited channel being the custodian of truth or the sole source of divine instruction. To go contrary to that runs directly into the face of God's Holy Word. And as we "keep his word" we "know that we are in him" (Verse 5). On the other hand, he who "does not keep his commandments is a liar and the truth is not in him" (Verse 4). These are serious matters.

It may be thought that I should take up in this discussion the subject of "apostolic succession." This is the idea that what was conferred upon the apostles was to be passed on officially by them to their successors, thus always leaving in the church a governing hierarchy tied by interlocking bonds back through the apostles to Christ Himself. Even the Church of England (Episcopalian) places great emphasis on this.

However, such discussion is hardly necessary, for when it is seen that the apostles were not really given any actual sacerdotal functions or absolute rule over God's church, then it will be recognized that there really is nothing authoritarian to be passed on to such supposed successors. Furthermore, no such "successors" are anywhere designated or referred to in Scripture. The twelve apostles filled an important place for that time and are to be honored for their zeal and steadfastness. That which has been passed on is the true faith, which has been passed on by multitudes of earnest believers from generation to generation down through the centuries.

What Is "Remitting" and "Retaining" of Sins?

Now to go a bit further, to some of those who seem to be trying to advise you refer to the promise made to St. Peter (Matthew 16), and to the committing to the apostles of the right to remit and retain sins (John 20). We may look at these briefly, but much of what we have already said applies to them.

Let us take up the latter one first since it is predicated upon receiving the Holy Spirit, which we have just considered. The words read, "He said unto them, 'Receive the Holy Spirit; whose sins you shall forgive, they are forgiven them; and whose sins you shall retain, they are retained'" (John 20:22, 23, Confraternity). To some this has appeared to be a most conclusive statement of authority; to others it is a most perplexing declaration. It therefore deserves looking into.

To begin with, let us assume for a moment, for the sake of argument, that this conferred upon the apostles a unique prerogative. Notice that in the wording nothing is said about successors to the apostles nor of anyone following them carrying on anything so unusual. Since no successors are indicated, and presumably it was something very special, that would point to it being just for that time and only for its immediate recipients. But it was not limited to certain ones, as we shall see, and therefore something of a more general nature, it becomes evident, was to be widely carried out.

Look at the actual wording. It begins, "He said unto them . . ." To whom does the "them" refer? Many have assumed that it was the apostles. But it does not say so, and this is the chief cause of misunderstanding in the whole matter. In the verses immediately preceding we find who the "them" is. Jesus was not merely addressing the apostles, who were a very limited group, but the passage speaks of those who were there as "the disciples," a larger, more general group. They are twice so specified here, in verses 19 and 20. Thus it was not the restricted number of the apostles that Jesus addressed. There is no suggestion in the records that it was just for them, as the term *apostle* is not used in this connection. This occasion took place on the evening of the resurrection day. The parallel passage in Luke already examined, where "those who were with them" are mentioned, again shows that Jesus spoke this to a larger gathering of common disciples. Therefore the whole thing is broader than some have recognized. As it is a general work for all disciples, we now look into how it applies to them.

What was that general work, or how can we determine what Jesus did mean by these words? In answer, the thing to be taken into account is how the disciples who were addressed actually did fulfill Jesus' directives. In the record of the early church period as contained in the New Testament we find the answer.

Those to whom this was committed never assumed the position of an elevated priesthood, they never pronounced "absolution" in the modern manner, they never assessed penance, they never

27

offered masses for souls (of the living or dead), they never used confessional boxes nor had anyone kneel before them. On the contrary, St. Peter forbad this last matter (Acts 10:26). Instead, they openly proclaimed or declared the forgiveness of all sins for those who would believe.

Observe the clear record. St. Peter shows the work with which they were charged. He says, *"And he charged us to preach to the people and to testify that he it is who has been appointed by God to be judge of the living and of the dead. To him all the prophets bear witness, that through his name all who believe in him may receive forgiveness of sins"* (Acts 10:42, 43). Thus they fulfill it as they "preach" or "testify" to that which brings about the "forgiveness of sins."

Similarly demonstrating that the preaching or proclaiming of the message is the means whereby forgiveness is effected, St. Paul says, *"Be it known therefore to you, brethren, that through him forgiveness of sins is proclaimed to you, and in him everyone who believes is acquitted of all the things of which you could not be acquitted by the Law of Moses"* (Acts 13:38, 39). You see how forgiveness of sins was tied in with the message preached, and the proclaiming of it was the fulfillment of Jesus' directives. Again St. Paul says that the sin question was resolved, not through priestly rites, but by God "entrusting to us the message of reconciliation" and thereby "not reckoning against men their sins" (II Corinthians 5:19).

That everything depended upon their preaching the wonderful message is also seen by Jesus' final word to His followers, where He said, *"Go into the whole world and preach the gospel to every creature."* And that is just what they did, as further stated, *"They went forth and preached everywhere"* (Mark 16:15, 20).

Showing that others beside the apostles fulfilled this, we read in Acts 8, "All except the apostles were scattered abroad. . . . Those who were scattered abroad went about preaching the word" (Verses 1, 4).

St. Peter, writing to "sojourners" scattered in many parts (I Peter 1:1), says, "You know that you were redeemed . . . with the precious blood of Christ" (Verse 18, 19), and "this is the word of the gospel that was preached to you" (Verse 25). The preaching, being received, accomplished everything.

St. Paul likewise speaks of *"the word of faith which we preach"* (Romans 10:8), and, *"It pleased God, by the foolishness of our preaching, to save those who believe"* (I Corinthians 1:21), and, *"You are being saved, if you hold fast, as I preached it to you"* (I Corinthians 15:2). All this, and yet not a word about priestly rites of absolution, or the like.

Bearing all this out, it is most significant to observe that neither the apostles nor any of Jesus' disciples speak in any of their writings of their power to directly remit or retain sins. If such absolute authority had been committed to them, it would have been one of their most important responsibilities and also one of the leading truths of Christianity. Can anyone imagine that they were so negligent or remiss in duty as to have failed to refer to it in their epistles, or in their preaching (faithfully recorded in the Acts)?

Going back to the parallel account in Luke 24, in which we saw that more than the eleven were involved, it is there further revealed how Jesus' words of promise were to be fulfilled. Continuing to speak to the same miscellaneous group, Jesus commissioned them by saying that *"Repentance and remission of sins should be preached in his name to all the nations, beginning from Jerusalem. And you yourselves are witnesses of these things. And I send forth upon you the promise of my Father. But wait here in the city, until you are clothed with power from on high"* (Luke 24:47-49). That which was to be "preached" would bring about the "remission of sins." That corresponds to the remitting or forgiving of sins in John 20:23. Then Jesus also said that "upon you," the whole group, was to come "the promise of my Father," by which they would be "clothed with power from on high." This corresponds, of course, with "Receive the Holy Spirit" of John 20:22.

Thus the whole thing becomes quite clear. Taken all together it was: (1) Nothing given to an exclusive group. (2) Preaching or proclaiming the forgiveness of sins was to fulfill it. (3) Disciples were to receive the power of the Holy Spirit to enable them to fulfill it.

Carrying Out Christ's Words

It may still be asked, what is meant by that which is designated as to "retain" someone's sins? Taking into view all that was said and all that was followed out, it becomes evident that remit or forgive conveys the idea of deliverance from the bondage and consequence of sins; retain means leaving one in a state where he continues bound by and under the dominance of sins. The whole verse could be paraphrased: *Whose soever sins you are the means of remitting by your preaching of the gospel, they are remitted; and whose soever sins you, after preaching the gospel, shall see retained through unbelief, they are retained.* The New Testament disciples did just that, they exercised the promised authority to pronounce or declare sins remitted or retained on the basis of their hearer's response to the message preached, the message of full and free forgiveness through Christ's finished work.

For those who have supposed that a priest can forgive sins, I would only say this: What a difference it would make if the Catholic Church really believed that! Those who maintain that priests were given authority to absolve from sins should be reminded that in the Catholic Church the priest assumes to forgive only one aspect of sins, and that only conditionally. He does not claim to absolve from the temporal punishments due for sins. True forgiveness is a very different thing; it is complete and absolute. Otherwise it really is not forgiveness at all.

In Scripture, forgiveness, remission, cleansing, purging and removal of sins are terms used interchangeably. When employed in respect to God's relation with man they indicate that which is entire and final. See Acts 3:19; 13:39; Colossians 1:14; 2:13; I John 1:7; Hebrews 10:17, 18; etc. If any priest on earth really fulfilled what is assumed to be found in John 20, there would be no need for any more masses, no need for prayers for the dead, no need of meritorious works in view of sins, no place for any purgatory. In connection with Jesus' words there is not the slightest thing said about either confession, penance, acts of contrition, making satisfaction, or absolution. God forgives sins and He forgives freely (Romans 3:24).

All of this ties in with our earlier discussion of the complete, once-for-all work of Christ. Don't you see that if satisfaction must be made by the penitent for the temporal punishment of sins, that degrades the sacrifice of Christ? It is to say that Christ's work was not sufficient, that God is not entirely satisfied with Christ's atoning death. I, as an individual, must make further satisfaction, and in view thereof must receive absolution from a priest—himself a sinner. For shame! Christ did not satisfy God's holy demands! But God says that in view of the completeness of Christ's one offering for sins He is forever satisfied, and therefore He will give full forgiveness to those who will claim it. God will never, *never* exact further satisfaction for sins already paid for. Be sure of that.

Oh how wonderful that we can receive at once, by faith alone, complete forgiveness and assurance of acceptance with God. Why not accept it for yourself and come to know the joy of full salvation?

4

Peter, the Rock and the Keys

The Promises to Peter and Their Fulfillment

Dear Teresa:

Thank you for your frank acknowledgement of the strength of the considerations which I have presented in my recent letters. You say, however, that the strongest and most important point yet has not been faced.

This is true. I intimated in my last letter that we might well take up this matter of Peter, the rock and the keys. You are aware that the common Catholic position is that the church was founded upon Peter personally, and that to him were given the keys of the kingdom. If this is the case it would settle about everything else involved. If Peter was the true and only foundation, and his successors were included, then others not related to that foundation are on false and perilous ground.

I have stood on more than one occasion, Teresa, beneath the imposing dome of Saint Peter's in Rome. It was said to be the greatest dome, not intermediately supported, of any edifice in the world, designed by no less a person than Michaelangelo himself. Gazing aloft, around the inside facing of the lofty cupola, attention is drawn to huge letters in Latin more than six feet high. They are the words of Jesus to Peter. They are, of course, conspicuously displayed there to emphasize the claim that the Christian communion centering in that place was founded—in virtue of those words—upon Peter.

It was late in Jesus' public ministry, after it was becoming evident that He was being rejected by the nation of Israel, that Jesus drew his disciples aside near Caesarea Philippi and asked them, first, as to whom men said He was. Upon being given the opinions then current, He asked them more specifically, "But who do you say that I am?"

Then we read, *"Simon Peter answered and said, 'Thou art the Christ, the Son of the living God.' Then Jesus answered and said, 'Blessed art thou, Simon Bar-Jona, for flesh and blood has not revealed this to thee, but my Father in heaven. And I say to thee, thou art Peter, and upon this rock I will build my Church, and the gates of hell shall not prevail against it. And I will give thee the keys of the kingdom of heaven; and whatever thou shalt bind on earth shall be bound in heaven, and whatever thou shalt loose on earth shall be loosed in heaven'"* (Matthew 16:16-19. Confraternity version of 1941).

By these words of Jesus, the Church claims to have been

founded upon St. Peter and to have received through him the keys to the kingdom and the power to bind and loose souls. That supposition is based upon this passage of Scripture—**which has probably been more abused and distorted than any other statement ever made by our Lord.**

The Church itself virtually stakes its claims upon this one utterance of Jesus as the primary and sufficient ground for its continued authority. For many years now, Catholic apologists have repeatedly referred back to these words as settling once and for all any challenge to its position.

In going over the reports of the Second Vatican Council, I noticed how, over and over, the Church refers to itself as the Church built upon blessed St. Peter, to its authority as grounded in the primacy of Peter, to Peter and his successors being given jurisdiction over Christ's entire Church, and to the Church of which St. Peter was appointed the visible head. For example, in the *Dogmatic Constitution On The Church,* we read, "The pope's power of primacy over all, both pastors and faithful, remains whole and intact. . . . The Roman Pontiff has full, supreme and universal power over the Church. . . . For our Lord placed Simon alone as the rock and the bearer of the keys of the Church, and made him shepherd of the whole flock." Again, in the *Decree On Ecumenism,* it is stated, "In order to establish this His holy Church everywhere in the world till the end of time, Christ . . . selected Peter, and after his confession of faith determined that on him He would build His Church. Also to Peter He promised the keys of the kingdom of heaven" (*The Sixteen Documents of Vatican II,* Daughters of St. Paul edition, pp. 132, 196).

The sweep of what is involved, supposedly based upon this text, is utterly astounding. By it defenders of the Church presume to stop the mouths of anyone questioning any aspect of the Church's authority or teaching. Theirs alone is the divinely established religious institution on earth, and that is the end of all controversy.

If this one point, however, is weak, the whole foundation is most shaky; and if it is shown to be really in error, the whole structure falls.

It is hard to believe that Catholic scholars have been entirely honest in dealing with this passage. But I will give them the benefit of the doubt and say that their thinking has long been conditioned on the subject, that they are so deeply involved in the Church that it is well nigh impossible for them to believe anything else than what their church reads into it. As another has said: "If our Lord's words will not bear the interpretation which Rome puts on them, the whole structure of Romanism is demolished. Rome dare not let the words as to the power of the keys, of binding and loosing, of retaining sins, be explained in any other than her own way; she dare not admit the possibility of their having any less extreme meaning; she must resort to every expedient to make them contain the unqualified transfer of Divine rights to herself, or the entire system which she has so laboriously built up falls to pieces" (Nichols, J. B., *Evangelical Belief,* pp. 156-157).

The passage in question, however, should be approached with honest candor. Only by facing it with an open mind can we be assured as to where the truth lies. Lest it seem that an attempt is being made to wholly downgrade Peter, let me here insert that we recognize and gladly acknowledge that running through the passage—*up to a point*—the Lord commends Peter for his bold confession. And truly He points to some future service which Peter is to render. But nothing more. Admittedly Peter was honored by the Lord. But there were limits to both the service he would render and to the honor he should receive. We do not want to deny Peter a deserving place, but neither do we want to go beyond what the Lord saw fit to grant His fallible servant.

It should also be pointed out that natural qualities of leadership do not in themselves constitute jurisdiction over others, nor does honor worthily bestowed constitute permanent supremacy. The former in each case, Peter had; both of the latter become the subject of our inquiry. Let us then turn to the words and see just what they **do** say and what they **do not** say.

Linguistic Considerations

The text should first be considered from the grammatical and linguistic point of view. Anyone who knows his Greek New Testament recognizes that this is not a clear and unmistakable statement of the church being built on Peter. Jesus did not say, "Thou art Peter and upon thee I will build my church." He could easily have said that, if that had been what He had meant. He did not say, "Thou are Peter and upon you, Peter, I build my church." He could have said that. Nor did He say, "Thou art a rock and upon you as the rock I will build." Neither do we find, "Upon this Peter I will build my church." He purposely avoided all such straightforward statements.

Since He did not at this point say anything so direct, He could elsewhere have easily clarified this statement and explained what it meant. But He did not. He left this declaration veiled and ambiguous, never further indicating Peter's foundational position, as will become evident. This statement, as it stands, then, must be more closely analyzed.

Notice the wording. Jesus said, "Thou art Peter, and upon this rock I will build my church" (both Confraternity and Douay). These English translations reveal a difference in the words "Peter" and "rock," and that difference is manifest in the original. But Catholics point out that the name Peter means rock. That is true only up to a point. Look in any standard Greek lexicon (I have checked it in many) and you will see that the word for Peter—*petros*—really means small stone, fragment of a great rock, a movable piece of rock; whereas the word used for "rock" is a bit different—*petra*—meaning great rock, imbedded or solid and massive rock. The one could be a building stone, the other the great ledge or quarry from which the building stone is hewn.

This difference is further borne out by observing that the two words are different genders. "Peter" is masculine (with its own

33

separate declension), whereas "petra" is feminine (with a feminine declension). The first has masculine modifiers, while the second is accompanied by feminine modifiers. All this shows a real difference. The verse actually stands this way: *"Thou* [masculine] *art Petros* [masculine], *and upon this* [feminine] *the* [feminine] *petra* [feminine] *I will build. . . ."* That precludes the latter part from relating to Peter. If Peter personally had been meant, it could have been either a masculine form of the word used in both parts of the sentence, or the feminine word for rock employed in both. But neither is employed throughout, and that rules out Peter being the one who was meant. Incidentally, the same differences appear in the Latin Vulgate, upon which the Catholic Church has so long depended.

Catholic apologists have been hard pressed to get around these undeniable differences. They have been forced to resort to a stratagem which is uncertain and which side-steps the facts. To get away from the force of the Greek, they try to shift the ground and claim that Jesus, in addressing Peter, actually spoke something else—Aramaic, or Syro-Chaldaic, or Syriac. In that native tongue, they say, there are not two such different forms, but that Jesus used the same term throughout: *Kepha . . . kepha.* But even this identity of the two words is uncertain, some believing that they may rather have been: *Kephas . . . kepha.* Actually, it is impossible to determine just what terms Jesus may have employed in speaking. Some believe He may have used none of those, but the Rabbinical Hebrew instead; others think He may have used the then widely employed Greek. Therefore it is a poor dodge to try to hide behind some uncertain, unprovable vernacular. That vain attempt is really a confession that the Greek leaves no question as to the difference between Peter and the rock.

The point of it all is that the only inspired text of which we have authentic copies is the Greek. No reliable copies of the Eastern Aramaic text have been in continuous use and come down to us. (If the Gospel of Matthew was originally written in Aramaic, as is often claimed, why did not the Church—supposedly the custodian of the Scriptures—preserve that all-important text?)

Nevertheless, the Catholic Church recognizes the Greek text as authentic and dependable. I have here a book entitled, *Rome and the Study Of Scripture: A Collection of Papal Enactments . . . Together with the Decisions of the Biblical Commission* (Sixth Edition, Revised, Grail Publications, 1958, Nihil Obstat, Imprimatur, etc.). In it we read, ". . . the Fathers, all ecclesiastical writers, and even the Church herself, from the very beginning, have used only the Greek text of the Gospel known under the name of Matthew as canonical, . . . it can be proved with certainty that the Greek Gospel is identical in substance with the Gospel written in the vernacular. . . ." (p. 126). Even venerable Bishop Challoner, in his introduction to Matthew in the official Douay-Rheims edition of the Catholic Bible, says, "As it was translated in the time of the Apostles into Greek, that version was of equal authority."[1] Let us, then, rest upon the Greek which is clear and decisive. Nothing at all is achieved by trying to avoid its force, as has so often been done. The Greek establishes both the differences in the meaning of the two words and the distinction in the genders and their modifiers.

This understanding is further fortified when it is called to attention that the words *"thou"* and *"this"* (in "thou art Peter, and upon this rock," verse 18) differ not only in gender, but also in both person and in case. (*Thou* is second person; *this* is third person; *thou* is a masculine personal pronoun; *this,* feminine, is demonstrative and used as an adjective.) While "this" does not fit in with *Petros* [Peter], it does point back to something antecedent, to the confession referred to by Jesus' statement, "flesh and blood has not revealed this unto thee" (Verse 17). It could read, "flesh and blood has not revealed this (the truth or Person confessed) unto thee . . . upon this rock I will build my church." Plainly, therefore, it does not point to Peter personally, but to the substance of the confession.

What, then, did Jesus mean?

Since, as we have seen, that upon which Jesus was to build His church was not a fragment or little stone (a *petros*), but a great, massive rock (a *petra*), it must point to something infinitely above Peter. And what, or who, is far greater than Peter? The answer, of course, is that it is the One whom Peter had just confessed, Christ Himself. This is abundantly borne out in further Scripture (I Corinthians 3:11: 10:4; I Peter 2:3-8).

The Keys Committed To Peter

At this point someone will be sure to ask, *But do not the words of Jesus which immediately follow show that all of this was addressed to Peter? Did not Jesus commit to Peter the keys and the power to bind and loose?*

In answer we say, yes, Jesus now shifts from the impersonal— the confession which shows that upon which the church is built —to the personal, the confessor. But a shift it is, a real change in construction, and the two phases of His address should not be confused.

We have no desire to depreciate the man Peter. Though at times he blundered miserably, he still possessed some notable qualities. He was bold, ready to speak out, a natural leader, a warm-hearted character. And when he realized he had erred, he was ready to show real sorrow of heart.

The use of the keys, to which Jesus referred, may be easily explained. Jesus here employed common Jewish usage which would be familiar to Peter and the other apostles, all of whom were Jews. The keys commonly stood as the token of a scribe, and of a stewardship committed to the possessor thereof (Luke 11:52).

---

[1] *In a more recent Catholic edition of the New Testament, the Douay Version, with Introduction and Notes by J. P. Arendzen, D.D., Ph.D.., M.A. (Sheed & Ward, 1947, Imprimatur, etc.), we find an even more conclusive statement:* "The Church guarantees that the Greek translation faithfully represents the Aramaic text" (Matthew. p. 1).

More directly, a key—*as is readily recognized*—is commonly used to open something, to make available entrance or access into something. The use of some such keys were Peter's reward for his ready confession. And he made good use of the keys.

On the eventful day of Pentecost, Peter initially opened the door of the visible church to the Jews when he preached his memorable sermon to the crowds in Jerusalem. The climax of his message came when he proclaimed the very same truth which was the substance of his great confession, that "this Jesus" is "both Lord and Christ" (Acts 2:36). Three thousand souls then entered through this newly opened door. From that point on the door was wide open to the Jews, and through the testimony of different ones "the number of the disciples increased rapidly in Jerusalem; a large number also of the priests accepted the faith" (Acts 6:7). But that particular door did not need to be opened again.

Peter's second use of the keys is seen where he opened another door—this time to the Gentiles. He had the honor of being the first to preach the gospel to other than Jews. In the house of Cornelius at Caesarea (Acts 10), the door was gloriously opened to non-Jews. A number of Gentiles, believing, were saved and received the Holy Spirit. That door, too, once opened, remained open. Thank God!

So crucial was this second incident that Peter later rehearsed it to his fellow apostles (Acts 11:1-18), and then before the whole assembly gathered in Jerusalem (Acts 15:7-11). The result was that it then helped to settle matters for new believers. The gospel being first proclaimed to each leading class, it could not again be first proclaimed. No further need was subsequently found to open any door. In fact, Peter, having fulfilled the use of the keys, is not so much as heard of once again (after the last reference cited) in the history of the church as recorded in Acts. His was a precedence only of historical order, strictly an inaugural work. That work, important as it was, was finished.

There was no earthly succession. Thereafter, the only keys of which we read are in the hands of the Lord Himself (Apocalypse 1:18). It is most significant that, in the Matthew passage, where Peter comes in, mention is made that "the gates of hell shall not prevail" against the church; whereas in the Apocalypse, the risen Christ says, "I have the keys of death and of hell." The same word for "hell" (hades) is used in both places. Therefore we conclude that now the keys of death and destiny are not found in any earthly ecclesiastical hands, but in Christ's alone.

The Binding and the Loosing

Following on, we come to the words about binding and loosing. These words are somewhat similar to the words in John 20:23 about remitting and retaining sins, which we have already analyzed. Very largely the same considerations apply here.

The wording here, however, is a bit different. Continuing His conversation with Peter, Jesus says, "and whatever thou shalt bind on earth shall be bound in heaven, and whatever thou shalt loose on earth shall be loosed in heaven" (Matthew 16:19). Since these words have been assumed to impart authority to the priesthood, or to give the hierarchy its position of jurisdiction, it is well to examine them.

It should be observed, first, that just two chapters further on in the same book, we find the same words addressed to all the disciples as a body. There is this difference, however, that where in the earlier reference the singular "thou" is employed (Matthew 16:19), in the second passage the plural is found (not so apparent in the English), here rendered "you," applying it to all the group (Matthew 18:18). This second statement, following so closely upon the first one (and found nowhere else), is quite evidently intended to explain and amplify the earlier one. The fact of the same thing being said to the whole group certainly indicates that Jesus did not want it thought that anything of an exclusive nature was bestowed upon Peter, and by him passed on through a limited channel of succession. It is something they were all to share in common.

It is rather significant that these two declarations about binding and loosing were never later alluded to by the apostles, nor appealed to by anyone in New Testament times after the church became established. Since there is no record in the later New Testament church of any special authority which might be associated with these words ever being carried out, the words evidently had peculiar reference to that time only.

The terms "binding" and "loosing" were used among the Jewish Rabbis who employed the designation "to bind" as to forbid, and the "to loose" as to permit (see theological encyclopedias, including the Catholic Encyclopedia). We must remember that the newly formed church was then composed of those with strong Jewish background.

It may well be said that the preceding reference to the "keys" is a figure. Similarly the binding and loosing are admittedly figurative terms, and by themselves this should eliminate them as a sound basis upon which to establish a permanent truth or practice. In fact, they are the third metaphor in a close succession of figures (rock, keys, binding and loosing). In *Who Is The Pope?* by M. D. Forrest (The Paulist Press; Nihil Obstat, Imprimitur, etc.), the author speaks of the keys as "the second metaphor used by our Lord" (p. 10), and then he says of the binding and loosing, "Yet another metaphor did Christ use" (p. 11). The more of this imagery that appears in the same connection, the less safe it is to attempt to use it as grounds upon which to build a doctrine frought with such momentous consequences. These were Jewish symbols, and unless otherwise explained, are uncertain groundwork for the Christian church after its establishment.

In the two statements about the binding and loosing, as that to Peter came first and then it was shortly given to all the apostles, so Peter was initially used, as we have seen, to declare the new plan of God first to the Jews (Pentecost), and then to the Gentiles (house of Cornelius). Then there followed similar widespread work of bringing all peoples into the church by the other disciples.

It has been thought that since such words were first addressed to Peter (Matthew 16), this gave him a precedence over the others to whom, so soon afterward, the same was committed (Matthew 18). But the fact is that in between these two occasions Peter neither showed any superiority to the others, nor did he exercise anything which indicated a higher position. The words were evidently first spoken to Peter because the use of the keys had just been referred to him, and this which so shortly followed would be an illustration of how it would be carried out by all of them.

Every possible place where Peter was the first to act has been brought to attention as evidence of his prior rights, as justification of his being prince of the apostles and head of the universal church. For example, Cardinal Gibbons says, "Peter . . . was destined to be the oracle which all were to consult. Hence we always find him the prominent figure among the Apostles, the first to speak, the first to act on every occasion" (*The Faith of Our Fathers,* p. 103). **This is just not so!** Very conveniently overlooked are places where other apostles were in certain instances ahead of Peter, or the first invloved.

For example, Andrew was the first of the apostles to be invited by Jesus to dwell with Him (John 1:38-41). That did not bestow upon Andrew any precedence or superority over others who might later find similar privileges.

Philip was the first apostle to be asked by Jesus about providing for the multitude (John 6:5-7); and when certain Greeks would see Jesus at Jerusalem, they came not to Peter, but first to Philip, who saw that they got to Jesus (John 12:20-23). These things did not give Philip an authority or priority over the others.

John, and not Peter, was "the beloved disciple" and the one who leaned on Jesus' bosom at the last supper. And it was to John, not Peter, that Jesus committed His mother at the time of His crucifixion.

What is entirely lacking in Scripture is any suggestion that Jesus, in first dealing with or speaking to someone, thereby gave that person a precedence or authority over others in the area of the matter involved. Peter is no exception to this. No intimation is anywhere found that Peter was placed above others because he was the first dealt with in any matter.

As we read the inspired history of the early church, recorded in Acts, we never find that either the apostles or anyone else ever quoted or referred to these words about binding and loosing as a basis for any ecclesiastical authority. Then, beside the Acts, we have the apostolic epistles, including St. Paul's, all of which are laden with a wide array of instruction for the early Christian churches, and never therein do we find these words alluded to, nor any intimation that Jesus ever conferred any unique prerogatives on anyone. Nor do we ever find in the New Testament any suggestion of the actual exercise of such functions as are supposed to be found here. In view of all this, reading into the words the interpretation of later days is going beyond the limits of a right understanding of Scripture.

If the idea is still entertained that there is delegated to Peter the authority to bind or loose from sins, it will only be necessary to glance at Peter's own example in this regard. In the eighth chapter of Acts we find Peter confronting a professed believer who became involved in sin deserving sharp censure. This was Simon Magus, who outwardly repented. Did Peter then forgive—absolve—him? Or, doubting the sincerity of his repentence did he hold over him the having of his sins "retained"? **Nothing of the sort!** On the contrary, he said (and notice carefully the wording), "Repent . . . and pray *to God*, that *perhaps* this thought of thy heart may be forgiven thee" (Acts 8:22 Confraternity; emphasis mine). Peter does not presume to pronounce forgiveness because it is beyond him to know if the man's heart is right with God. If the great St. Peter was not empowered to know if one could be forgiven, how much less an ordinary priest today?

The Church Fathers on This Text

We have thus considered the three leading elements in this conversation of Jesus with Peter: the matter of the rock, the keys, and the binding and loosing. We have seen that they fail completely to uphold the audacious interpretation placed upon them later by the Roman church. It is really a sad situation when so much has been staked upon a peculiar understanding of words which, under close scrutiny, are seen not to hold up. Tragic, indeed, when so many have so long assumed so much in these words, only to find it all an unwarranted assumption.

Some Catholic writers, however, still persist in setting forth sweeping claims in behalf of St. Peter, based upon the Matthew passage. Many books in defense of the papacy assert that the early church Fathers recognized Jesus' words as applying to Peter. Rome's followers have been led to believe that from the beginning the Fathers were agreed that the Roman Church was founded upon Peter as the rock. To such it will come as a surprise, if not a shock, to learn that this is far from true.

Teresa, I have here a number of source books which refer to and document the investigation of a celebrated Roman Catholic scholar, Launoy, who studied the church Fathers on this matter and tabulated the results. Of a list of sixty-eight ancient Fathers, he found only seventeen who thought the rock might refer to Peter (and even that without reference to succession of jurisdiction). The majority, forty-four, believed it referred to Peter's faith confessing Christ as Messiah and Son of God. Eight held that it referred to all the apostles equally; sixteen believed it referred to Christ Himself.

If, in practice, the church from the beginning recognized a Vicar of Christ on earth, it must also have recognized from the beginning the meaning of the text upon which that position was based. But this is not the case. If the current papal viewpoint had been firmly established in those early centuries, how could *any* of the Fathers have declared themselves otherwise? Only a small minority, however, leaned toward the Church's present contention. These facts invalidate her claims. It shows that there is certainly no "unanimous consent of the Fathers"—*the principle by which Scripture is supposed by the Church to be interpreted.*

The great St. Augustine, having expressed uncertain views, in his later years advanced his final opinion that the rock referred to Christ. Even some of the popes, or rather "bishops," of Rome (they didn't know they were "popes" then!) did not agree that it referred to Peter personally as the foundation of the Roman primacy (e.g., Gregory I).

The same diversity of opinion among the ancient Fathers was noted by Archbishop Kenrick of St. Louis, who was present at the Vatican Council of 1870. There was much disputation on the point at that Council, and then only after considerable pressure was it for the first time declared an essential dogma.

Now I think that you will agree that the more essential to the church a doctrine is, the greater the probability that it would be held to by all from the beginning. Amid the vicissitudes and weighty problems facing the early church, it is inconceivable that no appeal was made to Peter's seat of authority—if such there were—in those difficult early days. The matter regarding which of the varying interpretations held by the ancient Fathers is the true one is not so much the point, as is the demonstration that there was among them no common unanimity and that it was not the universal belief of ancient Christendom that the church was built on Peter.

It may further be said that if the text under consideration leaves serious doubt as to Peter being the rock, how much more questionable is any interpretation which not only finds Peter first among the apostles, but also finds in him infallibility; and not only that, but also sees those words as including the same for his successors!

Subsequent Confirming Evidence

It was intimated that further light is thrown on the promise to Peter by an examination of that which is subsequently revealed in the New Testament. For many thoughtful persons these considerations alone settle the matter. Since much space has been given to the all-important words to Peter, I will try to set forth only some high points of this additional evidence.

To begin with, go back to Matthew 16, where appear the words spoken by Jesus which have been examined. The very next thing recorded in that chapter is a stern reprimand given to the now supposedly elevated Peter: Matthew 16:21-23. Here we find that Jesus spoke of His own all-important impending death in Jerusalem. Peter then attempted to rebuke the Savior and to turn Him from that goal, thereby actually rejecting the doctrine of the cross, the emblem of which Rome has so exalted.

This is the only place on record where any disciple ever presumed to rebuke the Lord. Jesus responded by not only repulsing Peter in telling him to get behind Him, but He even applied to that disciple the awful epithet "Satan" (Verse 23)! Instead of being the foundation of that which Christ was going to build, Peter proved himself to be the most outspoken antagonist of it! A moment before, Jesus called him Petros (stone), of which much has been made; here He calls him Satan, most often overlooked.

What kind of a foundation for a church would such a satanically denoted individual be? Peter at once demonstrated himself to be no solid rock, no infallible leader for any ecclesiastical structure. He was given the severest reprimand ever individually administered by Christ to any of His followers. The gates of hell would not prevail against the church, but conversely, the ruler of that infernal realm appeared to prevail against Peter.

If Peter had just been raised to the place of supreme head of Christ's church, and if the others were supposed to have followed his elevated leadership, they would have plunged with him into grievous error and with him been worthy of similar censure. If the words about the rock and the keys were to have made Peter the supreme pontiff, they should, after this incident, have been reinstated or further elaborated to make them of any abiding significance. Instead, we find that they are not so much as alluded to again. This should close the case and settle the limited application.

Going on in the Gospel of Matthew, we come to the twentieth chapter. In this is recorded one of two incidents where there was a dispute among the apostles as to who was the greatest. Before looking specifically at these occasions, just consider the bare fact that *after* Jesus had presumably given Peter the primacy, the apostles seemed to know nothing about it and they questioned the matter among themselves.

Two points of significance grow out of this. First, if the promise given to Peter in the presence of the rest had been sure, there would have been no occasion for strife on the subject to begin with. They would have known who was their appointed leader.

Secondly, in view of their raising the issue, Jesus' own integrity would have obligated Him to clarify the matter once and for all. He should have indicated who was supreme, if any one of them was, or was yet to be. On the contrary, Jesus revealed no supremacy, no precedence at all.

Now, looking at Matthew 20, we see a request for a place of pre-eminence made in behalf of two of the apostles, James and John. Jesus should have handed out a rebuke for not recognizing that Peter had already been given the position of privilege and honor. Instead, He chides those making the request—not because they were seeking to rival Peter, but for even thinking of positions of prominence. Then, before the whole group, He said: *"You know that the rulers of the Gentiles lord it over them, and their great men exercise authority over them. Not so is it among you. On the contrary, whoever wishes to become great among you shall be your servant, and whoever wishes to be first among you shall be your slave"* (Verses 25-27).

This incident is also recorded in Mark, where the central phrase appears, "But it is not so among you" (Mark 10:43). Thus, unlike secular systems of authority, those active in Christ's church were to enjoy a humble equality and no one among them was to be supreme over the others.

An incident of similar import occurred as recorded in Mark 9:32-36 (33-37, K.J.V.; also in Luke 9:46-48). This also followed

41

Jesus' statement about the rock and the keys. Here Jesus asked the group what they had been "arguing about" on the way. Then we read, "But they kept silence, for on the way they had discussed with one another which of them was the greatest." If the initial statement of the Lord in regard to Peter is the charter of the papal claims, it is really amazing how the apostolic band, including Peter himself, seemed to be entirely ignorant of that fact. In view of their apparently knowing nothing about any such thing, either Jesus lacked the ability to express Himself clearly or the *will* to so express Himself. Can you accept that?

According to the Church, Jesus had already determined the matter which at this point was once more the subject of contention. Jesus again, then, at this stage should have corrected the group's faltering understanding.

Who was to have the place of prominence? Christ does not remind them that it had already been bestowed upon Peter. Instead, He takes them all to task for their unbecoming self-seeking. He puts a child in the midst to give them a lesson in humility and self-abasement. Entirely out of place among them all, Jesus said in effect, are such ideas as "primacy," "jurisdiction," "rule," "supremacy," "authority," and the like. The only pre-eminence that should be evidenced is the pre-eminence of humble service and faithful labor in the Father's vineyard. How utterly groundless, then, are insistent claims of any church to the contrary.

5

Two Other Petrine Texts

More Words to Peter, and Their Fulfillment

Dear Teresa:

I appreciate your patience in wanting to have before you the full data on Peter's place in the great drama of the Church. It *is* most significant.

I recently heard an aggressive Catholic, with a confident grin on his face, refer to Jesus having given Peter the responsibility to "feed the sheep" of His church. The implication was that non-Catholics are outside the true fold and cut off from Christ's blessings.

What we have already seen in the gospels fails to uphold such popular contentions. Defenders of Roman Catholic claims, therefore, have come around to assert that in Matthew 16 Jesus only gave Peter a promise of something which was to be subsequently bestowed upon him. They have found two texts, much later in the gospel records, which they have seized upon as meeting this need. These have been brought forth as the ultimate grounds which give Peter his unique position.

Incidentally, this is in reality a confession of the weakness of the labored arguments built up around the words about the rock and the keys.

Peter, it is now pointed out, was given a weighty responsibility when he was told to "strengthen thy brethren" (Confraternity), or "confirm thy brethren" (Douay), as found in Luke 22:32; and when he was ordered by Christ to "feed my sheep," in John 21:15-17. These two passages, together with the one in Matthew 16, constitute what have come to be known as "the three Petrine texts."

I find that the reports of the Second Vatican Council refer a number of times to these later texts. For example, in the *Decree on Ecumenism,* we read, "Christ . . . selected Peter, . . . and after his profession of love, entrusted all His sheep to him to be confirmed in faith (Luke 22:32), and shepherded in perfect unity (John 21:15-18)" (*The Sixteen Documents of Vatican II,* p. 196). Again they are seen, in the *Dogmatic Constitution on the Church,* in relation with the words, ". . . this is the infallibility which the Roman Pontiff, the head of the college of bishops, enjoys in virtue of his office, when, as the supreme shepherd and teacher of all the faithful, who confirms his brethren in their faith, . . ." (Ibid, pp. 135-136.)

If these two texts are supposed to bestow in final form that which was promised in Matthew 16, something is woefully lacking, for in neither of the texts is there any reference whatsoever to either rock, foundation, gates of hell, keys of the kingdom, or binding and loosing. How, then, can they possibly be the fulfillment of an earlier promise containing those elements?

The manifest circumstances, moreover, in connection with each of these later texts have been entirely overlooked, but when noted, throw a very different light on Jesus' words than that which has been assumed. These declarations had to do with the familiar incident of Jesus foreseeing and warning Peter that he would thrice deny Him before the cockcrowing.

"Strengthen Thy Brethren" Examined

The first one is in Luke 22:32, the heart of it being the words, "Do thou, when once thou hast turned again, strengthen thy brethren." These words Jesus spoke to Peter. In the use of this text, however, the context must not be ignored. As one reads on it will be seen, in verses 33 and 34, that Peter became arrogant and boastful, and that Jesus forewarned him of his fall, consisting of his cowardly and repeated denial of his Lord. It was for this reason alone that Jesus singled him out. In spite of this clear warning, Peter plunged headlong into his blatant denial—he fell into shameful apostasy.

It is fortunate that Jesus foresaw and made provision for his turning again, otherwise Peter might have succumbed to such remorse and despair as to have given up completely. That restoration, after such failure, is possible would indeed be an encouragement to his brethren—to the fallible apostles, as well as to all followers of Christ. This we see in the early chapters of Acts where Peter confirmed or strengthened his brethren, but after which he faded out of the picture and others became the dominant characters in the church.

Knowing Peter's instability and overconfidence, Jesus' words lay upon Peter, as one who had fallen and been restored, the obligation to encourage and strengthen others who might be prone to waver or go astray as he had. But to assist them in times of similar weakness is in no way akin to exercising authority over them. The other disciples momentarily forsook, but did not openly deny the Lord. Peter, having professed supreme loyalty, plunged to a lower depth than any of the rest (three times publicly denying the Lord with oaths or curses); therefore when he had "turned again" he was to be brought back to a plane *with* the others, not placed *above* them.

The word for *strengthen* (or confirm) in "strengthen thy brethren" is a term employed in the New Testament by various ones laboring among believers, not an exclusive function committed to Peter. In fact, it occurs far more often in reference to the work of others than in relation to Peter. For example, Paul is said to have "strengthened the churches" (Acts 15:41) and was "strengthening all the disciples" (Acts 18:23, same word), things not specifically said of Peter. Did this make Paul a pope?

Most remarkable of all, St. Paul, in writing to the church at Rome, said he wanted to come to them "to strengthen" them (same word; Romans 1:11; 16:25). This is rather astonishing as Rome was supposed to be Peter's special bailiwick—his peculiar fief. Yet there is no holding back or giving place to Peter in recognition of his prior rights there (or anywhere else)! It is most noteworthy that Paul anticipated that this important work in the Church of Rome would be his privilege and not Peter's. St. Peter's supposed special privilege completely breaks down.

The incident of Peter's boasting, fall and restoration indicates that he was far from being infallible—or even a reliable leader— for he, as no other, was to find need of being "converted" (Douay) or to "turn again" (Confraternity). And this was when he previously had been declared (supposedly) to be the rock. How unrock like! What a poor foundation would such a person be!

If Jesus' prayer for Peter (Verse 32a) did not prevent his falling into grievous error, how can it be imagined, in citing this passage, that it would guarantee that his alleged successors— those for whom the prayer was not even offered—would not likewise fall into error?

This second Petrine text, therefore, taken in the light of all the accompanying circumstances, rather than a proof of Peter's supremacy or that of any successors, is an argument against it.

"Feed My Sheep" Analyzed

The third and final text which is supposed to back up the assertion of Peter being that upon which the church was to be built, is found in John 21. This follows quite fittingly the passage in Luke, as it relates to the same matter of Peter's restoration after his shameful denials of his Lord.

After the resurrection Jesus confronted Peter with the thrice repeated question, "Lovest thou me?" Upon Peter's making an affirmative reply Jesus said, "Feed my lambs," and "Feed my sheep" (John 21:15-17).

The early church fathers concur in explaining this passage as a threefold questioning of Peter in order to make amends for his threefold denial. Drawing out from Peter three times his declaration of loyalty would have seemed to be unnecessary, but his previous loud professions of allegiance had so shortly before proven to be completely hollow when put to the test, that this appeared to be necessary. Thus the words to Peter merely assured him that he had not, by his denials, forfeited forever his position as a humble servant of the Lord.

It may fittingly be observed that we find that Peter "was grieved" (Verse 17) because Jesus had to draw out an answer from him three times. If Jesus' interrogation really led to an exalted position for Peter, it is hardly to be supposed that he would be grieved over such a procedure!

The record in John 21 continues. Peter, who had just been restored to whatever place the Lord intended for him, turns and, seeing John, asks a question in respect to what lies ahead for John (Verses 20, 21). If, as has been claimed, Peter was now assigned a position of oversight above the other disciples, it was a most appropriate question and fully within his province. But, quite to the contrary, Jesus responded by saying, "What is it to thee? Do thou follow me;" or, in other words, "That is none of your business; look after yourself" (Verse 22).[1] These are hardly the words to be spoken to one whose business it would be to superintend the others. John here was actually shown to be entirely independent of Peter and not accountable to him or anyone else except the Lord.

Jesus' words "Feed my lambs" have generally been taken to refer to training or teaching children or young Christians, and the "Feed my sheep" to properly instructing and leading adult believers. The latter phrase could hardly refer to jurisdiction over the pastors of the church, for in I Peter 5:1, 2, Peter himself delineated the feeding. He addressed the "presbyters," not being above them, for he speaks to them pointedly as "I, your fellow-presbyter" (Verse 1). Presbyters, himself included, are to "tend" —same word as *feed*—"the flock" (Verse 2). Therefore, to feed or tend the flock is no special prerogative of Peter. All the Lord's servants are to fulfill the same function. Paul, in the same way that Peter did, exhorted all presbyters or elders to "feed the flock" (same word, Acts 20:28). Thus, receiving a command to feed the flock does not make the one to whom it is extended a supreme ruler or place him in a position of jurisdiction over the whole church. Peter was no exception to this.

Light From Continuing Apostolic Activity

Even more decisive in regard to St. Peter's position is that which is revealed in the progressive history of the newly established church. We find in the New Testament books which follow the Gospels much disclosed as to the doings and position of various ones prominent in the apostolic church. All of this is most instructive. It is enlightening to follow through on Peter and see what actually *was* and *was not* exercised by him as shown by these later accounts. This will indicate whether or not we have rightly evaluated the passages observed in the Gospels.

Turning to the opening chapters of the Acts of the Apostles, we find Peter active in the early church. To some extent he even played a leading role and we give him due credit for it. That is in accord with what we said about his use of "the keys" in getting the church under way. But then note—*and this is important*—his prominence declines. He not only falls to a common level with the others, but, on occasion, is subject to them and challenged by them—far different from what would be expected of one who is the visible head of Christ's church and His "vicar" on earth.

While many Roman Catholic writers just assume, without real proof, Peter's continued leadership, some Catholic scholars are disturbed, to say the least, by this discrepency—this failure to

---

1 *The New American Bible,* translated by members of the Catholic Biblical Association of America (L. F. Hartman, et al, 1970), renders this passage in a most telling manner: "Jesus replied, 'how does that concern you? Your business is to follow me.' "

find Peter continuing in the place of prominence or manifestly exercising the position of jurisdiction. For example, Baron Friedrich Von Hugel, an erudite and brilliant gentleman of noble background, a loyal son of the Catholic church who wrote works of wide influence on Roman issues, evidently saw these difficulties in the later apolostic period. In *Some Notes On The Petrine Claims*, he frankly says, "I quite admit that parts of *Acts* and of St. Paul's Epistles *are* diffculties" (page 33, emphasis his). And again, "The primacy . . . requires to be, somehow or other, maintained through *Acts* and Epistles" (p. 80). We quite agree that many Catholic apologists have desperately "somehow or other" attempted to maintain that primacy. But let us look at the inspired record.

As an example, observe the statement in Acts 8, "Now when the apostles in Jerusalem heard that Samaria had received the Word of God, they sent to them Peter and John" (Verse 14). Notice here the very reverse of what we have been led to believe should have been expected. It wasn't Peter who sent and the others who complied. It was the apostles who sent and Peter accepted orders from them, submitting to their directives. He took the place of a subordinate.

On Roman principles Peter should have been the sender and not the sent. Peter, you see, did not remain in the place where the church was centered, occupying a seat of dignity and prestige and determining policy, sending out legates at his own will or in his name.

Then, in the eleventh chapter of Acts, we find that Peter, after another excursion from Jerusalem in which he had preached to and baptized Gentiles (chapter 10), was challenged upon his return by some in the Jerusalem church for what he had done. We read that those there still following Jewish custom "found fault with him" for his conduct (11:2, 3). He was forced to give an extended defense of his action. He did not rebuke his critics for questioning his doings, as he might have done had he been given supreme jurisdiction. No papal authority was yet recognized, nor was there any attempt to exercise any. Neither were those who called Peter to task accused of any insubordination or of failure to recognize Peter's place. In submitting his defense, Peter thereby admitted their right to question his conduct.

In Acts 15 a similar issue arose. The church at Antioch, disturbed by problems relative to Gentiles, decided to send Paul and Barnabas to "go up to the apostles and presbyters at Jerusalem" about this matter (Verse 2). Notice that it was not to any one among the apostles, as the highest authority, to whom they were sent. And "presbyters" (elders) were included as well as apostles. In fact "the whole church" (Verse 22) was involved in resolving the issue.

Then, when they came together, Peter played only a minor role. It was only after "a long debate" that Peter spoke at all (Verse 7), merely giving a report. But this did not end it. Barnabas and Paul were next heard. And finally St. James who, rather than Peter, evidently was the moderator, spoke at length and then terminated the discussion and gave his decision, saying, "Therefore my judgment is. . . ." (Verse 19). The assembly's determination followed the lines of this pronouncement of James.

Letters were sent out giving the decree, not in the name of any supreme pontiff, but as that which was "arrived at by the apostles and presbyters" (16:4). You see, Peter did not call, convene or summon the council (they met by common consent), preside over it, pronounce the final decision, nor extend his special approval to that decision. There was yet no "vicar of Christ" on earth, nor any single "visible head" of the church.

Now we come to the point of greatest significance in the book of Acts. As we have already mentioned, this which we have just considered is the last that is heard of St. Peter in the divinely recorded history in Acts. He is not so much as mentioned again in the thirteen following and highly significant chapters. This is even more remarkable as that record closes in the much discussed city of Rome itself.

Paul's Defiance of Peter

In respect to St. Peter's conduct, St. Paul's testimony, which comes down to us in his inspired writing, is most illuminating. It underscores and makes even more emphatic what we have seen in the Book of Acts.

At various times in church history, certain papal advisers have counseled courses of action different from that suggested by the pope. But what happened in Antioch (Galatians 2) in respect to Gentile relationships went far beyond anything of that nature. Paul not only rebuked Peter to his face in front of a whole assemblage, but then later put it on permanent record for the whole world to read. Indeed, Paul seemed a bit proud of his stand against Peter, with no trace of fear in rebelling against recognized authority.

Peter had no part in founding the church at Antioch. Paul, however, arrived there early, building up the church, and there the believers were first called Christians (Acts 11:19-26). Some time later Peter showed up, taking a Jewish position contrary to full Gentile freedom from Mosaic regulations. Paul says, "I withstood him to his face, because he was deserving of blame" (Galatians 2:11). Just think of anyone, even an apostle, withstanding to the face one who was supposed to be the supreme pontiff, and then adding, "he was deserving of blame"! Paul further records, for all to know, that Peter and his clique were "not walking uprightly according to the truth of the gospel," and so Paul spoke his reproof "to Cephas [Peter] before them all" (Galatians 2:14). Imagine publicly giving "the holy father" such a reprimand! But that is the clear record and is entirely destructive of Romanist assumptions. Peter was the only one of all the apostles who was ever thus "withstood" or "blamed" by another apostle.

And, be it marked, the Christian church has ever since followed the position taken by Paul rather than that taken by Peter. Peter's policy would have proven fatal to the whole future of Christianity. Plainly, Peter was not recognized, and happily so for the church, as having any supreme status. He not only lacked the power to propound edicts (papal decrees), but he actually erred and was guilty of serious misjudgment.

Had Peter been conscious of his superior status he would have put Paul in his place very shortly, and had the others recognized Peter's position they would have backed him up in this. But we find nothing of the sort. The church was saved from future peril by Paul's being able to rightly discern the will of the Lord and by his courage in resisting Peter's narrow and mistaken viewpoint. Had Peter prevailed here he would have done the opposite of what would have "strengthened his brethren" (Luke 22:32).

In that Galatian passage (chapter 2), it is also interesting and significant to note that the cause of Peter's downfall (temporary, we trust) was that he actually gave way to James as to a superior. We have already seen that James presided at and gave the decision in the Jerusalem council (Acts 15). Peter evidently recognized James as one having a higher position. It says that Peter, "before certain persons came from James," ate with Gentiles; but after the legates from James arrived, Peter, "fearing" their influence, gave place to them and thought it best "to withdraw and to separate himself" (Galatians 2:12). Thus the man supposed to be the rock switched back and forth, engaging in "dissimulation," as verse 13 puts it (the original word means *hypocrisy*). And this he did being influenced by others rather than standing on any rock-like primacy he himself might have had.

Other evidence is forthcoming that St. Paul recognized no superior whatsoever. Some Roman Catholic apologists have tried to make something of the statement in Galatians 1:18, where Paul says, "I went up to Jerusalem to see Peter, and I remained with him fifteen days." But note that this was three years after his sojourn in Damascus where he had been preaching (same verse). And a statement right in this connection is very conveniently overlooked where, immediately preceding, Paul says that he took up his mission to "preach him [Christ] among the Gentiles, immediately, without taking counsel with flesh and blood, and without going up to Jerusalem to those who were appointed apostles before me" (Galatians 1:16, 17; See also 2:11, 12; 1:1). Not being one of the original apostles, it might be thought that Paul should have received his commission (as nowadays) through the ecclesiastical establishment. But there is no evidence of such an authorative establishment, rather the contrary.

As to Paul's relation to other apostles—including the mighty St. Peter—he says, "I regard myself as nowise inferior to the great apostles" (II Corinthans 11:5), and "In no way have I fallen short of the most eminent apostles" (II Corinthians 12:11). There is no graded hierarchy here.

Peter Slips From First Place

Earlier mention was made that every place in the Gospels where Peter was first or seemed to be prominent has been paraded as evidence of his priority, even though in other instances other apostles were the first to act. In addition to this,

Catholic writers have asserted that in naming the apostles, Peter is always listed first. That was true in the Gospels and opening chapters of Acts, in accord, as we said, with Peter's playing a prominent part in getting the newly formed church under way. But the keys once having been used to open the doors of Christian privilege to Jews and Gentiles, that distinction no longer held. If it was not something which was to remain with Peter, how could that which ceased give him permanent status or be passed on to any successors?

Look again at the second chapter of Galatians. One more pertinent point may be seen there. In the ninth verse, Paul says, "When they recognized the grace that was given to me, James and Cephas [Peter] and John, who were considered the pillars, gave to me and to Barnabus the right hand of fellowship." Note here that not Peter, but James, is named first. Peter rates second, being in the middle. What he does is merely equal to or in joint action with others.

But Peter is slipping fast. In I Corinthians 9:5 he appears to have moved down to third rank. We read, ". . . as do the other apostles, and the brethren of the Lord, and Cephas" (Compare 1:12). First place is his no longer. Peter quite evidently is no permanent ecclesiastical superior, is not chief of the apostles, nor is ranked first in the church.

Who Held the Precedence In Rome?

Not having conferred with flesh and blood (Galatians 1:15, 16), Paul went forth as commissioned by Christ alone (Galatians 1:1, 11, 12; Ephesians 3:2, 3, 7; Titus 1:3), and planted churches throughout the Roman empire. How blind some people can be to plain facts! As others before him, from whom he evidently takes his cue, the previously quoted Baron Von Hugel dares to say, "Paul entered later upon the work begun by Peter, and built on the foundation he had laid" (*Some Notes on the Petrine Claims*, p. 43). That is exactly what Paul said he would *not* do. He said, "But I have not preached this gospel where Christ has already been named, lest I might build on another man's foundation" (Romans 15:20).

This last statement of Paul's, be it observed, was written to the believers in Rome. Paul tells them that he wanted to come to them "that I may impart some spiritual grace unto you to strengthen you," and "that I may produce some results among you," and then, "I am ready to preach the gospel to you also who are at Rome" (Romans 1:11, 13, 15). Yet, telling them that he would not build on another man's foundation, he would not have entertained that purpose of ministering to them if Peter had already been or was on his way there.

The Catholic Church says Peter was there and became the first bishop in Rome. However, Paul, in the last chapter of this epistle to the Romans, mentions twenty-seven Christians by name, extending salutations—yet refers in no way to Peter. Either Peter was not there or Paul deliberately slighted him—which is unthinkable if Peter were head of the church in that place.

50

A few years later Paul himself arrived in Rome. St. Luke records details of his reception there (Acts 28), and still no reference to Peter, who would have been the most outstanding Christian personage in that city. And Luke did not hesitate to give full prominence to Peter in the first twelve chapters of that record (Acts), and did recount Peter's labors in Jerusalem, Samaria, Lydda, Joppa, Caesarea.

Then, while in Rome, Paul wrote four epistles in which he mentions by name many Christians who were there (Philippians 4:21, 22; Colossians 4:10-14; Philemon 23, 24). Still there is no reference to Peter. He did include Timothy as being there, in extending greetings to those to whom he wrote (Philippians 1:1; Colossians 1:1, 2); then why not something about so important a person as Peter? Furthermore, Paul mentioned to the Colossians certain ones like St. Mark who helped him there, and added, "These *only* are my fellow-workers in the kingdom of God; they have been a comfort to me" (Colossians 4:11). Yet there is not the slightest mention of Peter.

Later, during his final days of imprisonment in Rome, Paul again referred by name to some who forsook him, others who departed from the city, and then he says in the last words coming from his pen, "Only Luke is with me" (II Timothy 4:11). Where was Peter? The answer, most evident, is that he was not at Rome. Paul anticipated his impending martyrdom (II Timothy 4:6-8), but he does not commend believers to any seat of supreme authority to which they can look in those troubled times for solace or guidance. Since Paul was so prominently mentioned in Holy Scripture in connection with Rome, why not some—even a minor reference—to Peter if he played any role at all in that place? There is no clear answer by those contending for Peter's suzerainty in that city.

Peter In Further Eclipse

Following St. Peter's decline, St. Paul's ministry becomes the leading ministry in the apostolic church. Paul gives more positive directives to the churches than any one else, including him who was admonished by Jesus to feed the sheep. In counseling the churches, Paul never refers them to the position or authority of anyone who is Christ's vice-regent on earth. For example, in a final and impassioned meeting with the leaders of the Ephesian church (Acts 20: 17-36), Paul warns them of both forthcoming heresy and of disunion; but he does not tell them that by holding fast to the supreme pastor and visible head of the church they would be safeguarded from these deadly pitfalls. Yet he added that he kept back nothing that would be profitable for them and that he had given them the whole counsel of God (Verses 20, 27).

Along the same line, St. John in his three epistles speaks of false doctrine and other dangers confronting the believers, but he never presses upon them the refuge to be found in an infallible teacher and guardian of the faithful who would, if clung to, see them through their perils.

The same may be said of the epistles of St. James and St. Jude: instruction, warning and broad appeal. Yet there is no referral to any supreme source of truth on earth or guide to the faithful. A very serious oversight, indeed, if there had been any such deciding voice from an earthly seat of authority; yea, in that case, an utterly inexcusable omission.

Accordingly, if the Lord had meant to say that Peter more than others was to be the abiding foundation of the church, why did all the other apostles and leaders of that day ignore the fact? **That question is fatal to Rome's claims.** And remember that the bulk of these epistles, as well as the Acts, was written *after* Peter was supposed to have taken his seat and exercised authority as chief shepherd in the imperial city.

You see, my friend, Peter himself must never have thought that Jesus' words gave him any permanent supremacy. He never claimed primacy nor to be the visible head of the church, even where such claims would have been very convenient or useful to the situation. He could, if such had been his rights, have readily resolved issues, settled questions, and also avoided a degree of personal embarrassment. He could thereby have spared the fledgling church much uncertainty and needless controversy. But no trace of such final authority is anywhere found.

Teresa, when I was in Rome a number of years ago, my brother came into our hotel room one day jubilant in that he had secured a permit or credentials for us to be included in an "audience" with the Pope at the Vatican. Upon inquiry into the requisites for such a meeting, I learned that we were required, upon being presented to the Pope, to get down upon our knees and make a gesture of obeisance. I declined to go. **How un-Petrine is such a practice!** In Acts 10:25, 26, we read that Cornelius, upon Peter's entrance, "falling at his feet, made obeisance to him. But Peter raised him up, saying, 'Get up, I myself also am a man'." The Pope never does that nowadays with visitors; rather the opposite.

Peter's Own Testimony

Peter nowhere made claims to be more than his fellow men. In the record which he left us in two epistles he never mentions or implies a place of superiority. And Peter was never backward in asserting himself.

The final proof of his position of equality comes to us from Peter's own and only statement on the subject. In I Peter 5:1, he says, "Now I exhort the presbyters among you—I your fellow-presbyter. . . ." The highest designation he gives himself is that of a common fellow-presbyter. The term rendered "fellow-presbyter" is in the original *sumpresbuteros,* which means joint-presbyter, or co-presbyter. Thus Peter put himself on a level or on the same plane as other presbyters (elders) or Christian workers.

Then Peter tells them to "tend the flock" which is among them, "not by constraint . . . nor yet as lording it over your charges" (Verses 2, 3). Still further he adds, rather than a claim for himself (as so many popes have made), a reference to Christ alone as "the Prince of the shepherds" (Verse 4; compare 2:25). But he never took any title approximating that for himself.

It is useless to plead, as has been done, that Peter's great humility kept him from asserting his prerogatives. That would not have been characteristic of Peter. Nor have later popes ever hesitated in putting forth their claims. If Peter had been given a position of authority by the Lord it was his solemn duty to make that very plain. Concealing the matter would have constituted dereliction of responsibility. And since successors are presumed to have been included, declaring it would have saved the church through the centuries untold perplexity, controversy and divisiveness.

Summary

To summarize, Roman apologists have picked out here and there statements from the Gospels or early chapters of Acts, putting them together to make it seem to present a formidable case for St. Peter. But the Church through the years has not encouraged the reading of all the Word of God *as it is*. If passages and incidents to which I have called attention were interspersed between those distinctive of Peter, they would have thoroughly counterbalanced or neutralized his distinctiveness and, in fact, as the record continues, show that his occasional prominence disappears and that other leaders gain the ascendency.

Teresa, we have carefully examined the Scripture texts which have been regarded as the charter of the Church. But upon closer study they have been found to be devoid of any specific charter or permanent authority for an organized church. Quite the contrary, there is wholly lacking any clear evidence that Jesus gave any authoritarian position to any line of succession starting with St. Peter.

We saw that St. Paul had great prominence and influence in the early church. But no one has suggested that Paul handed anything on to a limited line of successors. And neither does St. Peter, useful as he was, show evidence of having had anything to hand on to a specific line of successors any more than did St. Paul.

The implications of these conclusions are most far reaching. If the keystone is removed, the whole arch collapses. In reality, then, there is no need to weigh other matters predicted upon the basic assumption of Peter's primacy. The supposed final authority in all matters is actually no authority at all.

The realization of this turn of events might cause some folk to give up in despair. Having placed faith for so long in a system which is found to have no basis in fact might lead to the casting aside of all belief and leave one in complete skepticism. (Some have gone that way.) But that is not at all necessary. Turn in faith to God alone. Trust Christ and go directly to Him. He will speak peace to your soul and give abiding spiritual assurance. I am a member of a particular church, but I plead for no organized church or earthly denomination. I plead for Christ alone, in whom can be found all that the soul desires or needs. Thank God for the plain and simple means of salvation which He has made accessible to all, and for the full provision for the Christian life which is within the reach of all who will avail themselves of it.

6

Direct Access to God and True Worship

How Is God to Be Approached and Worshiped?

Dear Teresa:

We have seen that there is really no basis for assuming that St. Peter or any presumed successors of his were the foundation of the Church, or were given absolute jurisdiction over it. Now, you ask, *who then is to perform for the faithful the services necessary in approaching God?* Some agency, you say, should be able to administer properly those authentic priestly functions which are essential for a right relation to and worship of God.

But such needs, Teresa, seem apparent only to one who has not yet clearly grasped the heart of New Testament truth. The whole underlying basis of the New Covenant is involved here. It is a covenant which supersedes, surpasses and supplants the Old Testament covenant with its priests and ritualism (see the book of Hebrews, chapters 7 through 9; etc.).

As I have become acquainted with and talked to many sincere Roman Catholics, I believe the major premise of their whole religious outlook is that the Church as an institution is very necessary in their approach to God. They assume without question that the Church is in existence for this very reason—to not only point the way, but to be the **very means** through which one may find God's saving grace. To question this would place these dear folk in a state of apprehension and fear of losing what they think is the only truly ordained means of gaining that which is necessary to the salvation of the soul.

It would seem to such earnest people a shocking thought—really almost blasphemous—to suggest that each soul may approach God directly, alone and unaided. Yet that is what we actually find in the New Testament. **This is very important!** God has plainly declared that nothing—nothing at all—should come between the soul and Himself. This will be quite a revolutionary thought to many.

Let me say that by direct approach to God I do not mean merely praying to God or crying to Him for mercy. I mean that, as far as receiving the full forgiveness of sins and the complete salvation of the soul is concerned, no human institution or earthly agency plays any necessary part—not even a supposedly divinely ordained Church. Of course, those who preach the gospel and tell of the free grace of God may serve a very useful purpose. But any soul learning of Christ's work in its behalf may go directly to God and receive immediately all that could be desired for that soul's eternal welfare. Neither does such a redeemed soul need any functionary to keep him in right relation to his God.

Can this really be shown to be true?

Yes!

In the first place, we have already seen that no exclusive or tightly constituted church organization was established upon the apostles or upon St. Peter, or provided for in any supposed successors of theirs. That alone would show that nothing of an on-earth establishment is necessary for men's spiritual welfare, for, if it had been, God would have declared it in unmistakable terms in His Word.

In the second place, we have also seen that God freely forgives all sin of those who really come to Him and who accept the finished atonement which He provided in His Son. That being the case, nothing else of any kind is in any way needed in order for one to get in right relation to God.

Scripture and the Direct Approach to God

Now, how do we know with assurance that no secondary agency has any place in standing between us and God? Can we be certain that no priestly functions or sacramental channels are required when it comes to having the problem of our standing before God taken care of?

Yes, the Word of God makes this clear also. That is, aside from seeing that there is no authoritarian church and that full forgiveness is immediately available from God, we further find our direct approach to God set forth in Scripture. Let us look at it.

When we considered earlier the once-for-all work of Christ, we turned first to the New Testament book of Hebrews where we saw that truth set forth so plainly. This additional truth is also very clear in that book.

In Hebrews 10:19-22 (Confraternity), we read, "Since then, brethren, we have confidence to enter the Holies in virtue of the blood of Christ, a new and living way which he inaugurated for us through the veil (that is, his flesh), and since we have a high priest [Christ, 8:1; 9:11] over the house of God, let us draw near with a true heart in fullness of faith, . . ."

Notice how this is addressed to "brethren," that is, in the New Testament, common believers, not clergy; and then it says "we" —all of us—have "confidence to enter," and therefore "let us draw near." We enter or draw near "the Holies," that is "not . . . a Holies made by hands, . . . but into heaven itself . . . before the face of God" (9:24). The "new and living way" means it is new because it is not by means of human priests, as was the old.

Again, in Hebrews 4:16 we read, "Let us therefore draw near with confidence to the throne of grace, that we may obtain mercy and find grace to help in time of need." And "the throne of grace" refers to that which is in God's presence "in the heavens" (8:1, 2).

In the next New Testament book we find the same theme. James 4:6-8 says, "God gives grace to the humble. . . . Draw near to God, and he will draw near to you." No secondary instrumentality is at all implied.

The first chapter of the next book, I Peter, shows how we may "invoke him as Father," and that He, the Father in Heaven, "without respect of persons" judges each one (I Peter 1:17). That means, since God is no respecter of persons, that neither priest, prelate or pontiff has any more standing before Him than anyone else. (For other references on God being no respecter of persons, see Romans 2:11, Ephesians 6:9, Colossians 3:25.) As a matter of fact, St. Peter, who wrote this, had himself to learn this truth by an impressive lesson (Acts 10), in consequence of which he was impelled to declare openly, "Now I really understand that God is not a respecter of persons" (Verse 34).

Later this lesson came back on Peter's own head, and St. Paul spoke in similar terms about Peter and his associates when, in Galatians two, Paul says, "What they once were matters not to me; God accepts not the person of man" (Verse 6); and for that reason Paul could say, "Now to these we did not yield in submission, no not for an hour" (Verse 5). Think, my friend, of all that is indicated in the divinely inspired statement, "God accepts not the person of man." You and I have as much standing before Him as anyone else, and we can approach Him just as confidently.

Going on with our main theme, in the second chapter of I Peter we are actually commanded to "Draw near to him" (Verse 4). It does not say draw near to an altar, or to some intermediary, but to draw near to God Himself. The thought of this might make some persons tremble, but remember, God loves us, loves each one of us, looks with favor upon us as individuals, and even longs for us to come to Him (Ezekiel 33:11; Romans 10:21; Revelation 22:17).

Let us look further into this subject. I call extended attention to it for two reasons: because it is so important, and also because it has been so neglected and so little appreciated.

In his epistles, St. Paul was led to present the same wonderful truth. In Romans 10, we read, "For there is no distinction between Jew and Greek, for there is the same Lord of all, rich towards all who call upon him. 'For whoever calls upon the name of the Lord shall be saved'" (Verses 12, 13). Thus we are to call upon "Him," and no one else is ever suggested as the object of our appeals or as standing between us and that object.

Again, in Ephesians we find the statements, "Through him [Christ] we both have access in one Spirit to the Father. Therefore, you are now no longer strangers and foreigners, but you are citizens with the saints and members of God's household" (2:18, 19); and, ". . . Christ Jesus our Lord. In him we have assurance and confident access. . . ." (3:11, 12). These statements were written to and included ordinary believers, even young Christians. Read the entire passages and you will see the full force of that which is set forth.

Now observe some of the wonderful words of Jesus in the Gospels. words similarly revealing how anyone can go directly to Him, needing no one to stand in between.

In John 7:37, Jesus' invitation is, "If anyone thirst, let him come to me and drink." Notice He said, "Come to Me," not to the church, or to the clergy, or to anything or anyone else. Similarly, in John 10:9, He says, "I am the door. If anyone enter by me he shall be safe." Again, in John 14:6, He says, "I am the way, . . . No one comes to the Father but through me." Oh, let us just take it all at face value and act upon it.

The Church's Teaching

But see what the Catholic Church says. I have here a book, one of "The Truth of Christianity Series"—this one indicated as "A Textbook for Colleges and Universities"—by Charles G. Herzog. S. J. (Imprimatur, Patric Cardinal Hayes, Archbishop of New York), entitled *Channels of Redemption*. Note the significant title. That conveys its teaching. Redemption can be applied to us only through specific, authorized channels. And those channels are in Church hands alone; the clergy control them.

This book speaks of "the seven Sacraments, the seven channels of grace. . . . The Sacraments carry Divine grace to men. The Church . . . rules our actions . . . but its greatest work is to bring life to us. . . ." (p. 4). Again, "We are not free to choose our own way of finding out what Christ revealed; we must learn His revelation from His Church. How, then, can we discover for certain whether or not there are Sacraments of grace? From the teaching of His Church" (p. 10).

And what is given as proof of all this? On the last page quoted, we read, "Christ speaks today through His own Church. He says concerning that Church, 'He that heareth you, heareth Me' (Luke 10:16)." Now that text is very interesting proof. The book says Christ spoke the words quoted "concerning that Church." Yet the amazing thing is that the church is not mentioned in that chapter, nor, in fact, anywhere in the whole book of Luke!

That same text, Luke 10:16, is similarly quoted for the Church's authority in Cardinal Gibbons' celebrated book, *The Faith of Our Fathers* (p. 318). It makes one tremble to think of what judgment such men are under who distort this and similar Bible texts. Yet, even in the pronouncements of the recent Second Vatican Council, this same text is similarly cited as proof for the following statement: "The Sacred Council teaches that bishops by divine institution have succeeded to the place of the apostles, as shepherds of the Church, and he who hears them, hears Christ, and he who rejects them, rejects Christ and Him who sent Christ." And at the end of that sentence the reference to Luke ten is appended. (*The Sixteen Documents of Vatican II*, Daughters of St. Paul edition, p. 130). Now, not only is the Church not mentioned at all in this connection, but neither are the terms "apostle" or "bishop," to which they refer, found in this chapter. And it was not the twelve whom Jesus sent out in the incident involved, but a larger group, the seventy to whom the words were addressed. So you see how utterly misapplied this text is! Yet that is a sample of how the Church tries to establish its authority.

But return again to the book, *Channels of Redemption*. We read further, "The prime purpose of the Sacrament of Holy Orders . . . is to confer on certain selected persons the spiritual power of sanctifying others. These selected persons sanctify others by bringing to them the means of grace; by the administration of the Sacraments they direct the flow of sanctifying grace into the souls of men" (p. 172). We also find the statement, "Holy Orders is the Sacrament which confers on certain members of the Church this power of dispensing grace through the sacraments" (p. 173). Now, if you have read your New Testament to any extent, you know that all of this is utterly foreign to its teaching.

The same book also says, "The priest . . . offers a real Sacrifice. The priest may have, in addition to this power, other spiritual powers; he may . . . absolve sins" (p. 174). Then it says that priests "were set apart from men, and made representatives of men before God" (p. 175). Do you see how this flatly contradicts all that we have seen in Scripture about nothing being between the soul and God?

Some of Cardinal Gibbons' expressions along this line are even more startling. He says, "The Priest . . . to the eye of faith is exalted above the angels, because he exercises powers not given even to angels." And, "Hundreds are sustained by him in spiritual life, and leave the Church depending on him. . . . I can say of every Priest what Simeon said of our Lord, 'This man is set for the fall and the resurrection of many in Israel.' Not only are Priests the ambassadors of God, but they are also the *dispensers of His graces* and almoners of His mercy. . . . To them alone He gave the power to forgive sins." And, finally, "The Priest should be like those angels whom Jacob saw in a vision, ascending to heaven and descending therefrom on the mystical ladder. . . . He ascends to draw at the Fountain of Divine grace, he descends to diffuse those living waters among the faithful." (*The Faith of Our Fathers,* One Hundred and Tenth Revised Edition, pp. 317, 319, 326, emphasis his.)

Other highly regarded authorities make exorbitant claims along similar lines. O'Brien, in *The Faith of Millions,* says, "The sacraments serve as so many channels through which the graces and blessings of Redemption reach the soul of each individual. . . . The Church may be said to be the extension of the Incarnation and the application of its fruits to the needs of individual human souls" (p. 159). You see, he uses that term "channels" again. And on the next page he has a full-page illustrated diagram designated, "The Sacraments Channels of Grace," showing at the cross a great "reservoir of grace" from which seven streams flow to the seven depicted sacraments. Finally, speaking of the priest's power over these sacraments, he says, "No wonder that the name which spiritual writers are especially fond of applying to the priest is that of '*alter Christus.*' For the priest is and should be *another Christ*" (p. 269).

Equally amazing is the power claimed for the sacraments themselves. The previously referred to volume, *Handbook of the Christian Religion* (Wilmers and Conway), says, "The sacraments *effect* grace by their own virtue. . . . The sacraments not only signify, but *effect grace.* . . . That those sacraments which *produce the supernatural life* in the soul confer sanctifying grace is manifest. . . . The sacraments effect grace by their *own inherent power* in virtue of the sacramental act itself. The sacramental rite itself is the cause of grace" (pp. 305, 306, 307, 308, emphasis in original).

We find all of this and much more in spite of the clear statement of Scripture, "For there is one God, and one Mediator between God and men, himself man, Christ Jesus" (I Timothy 2:5). When man takes unto himself that place which Christ has declared is His, it is more than arrogance, it is outright defiance toward the divinely decreed plan.

Scripture also says, "For there is no distinction, . . . They are justified freely by his grace through the redemption which is in Christ Jesus" (Romans 3:22-24). You see, justified "freely" and not through binding channels.

The Second Vatican Council, contrary to the thinking of many, seems not to have toned down the extravagant claims which we have noted. In its reports, we read, "The Sacred Council . . . teaches that the Church, now sojourning on earth as an exile, is necessary for salvation. . . . Whoever, therefore, knowing that the Catholic Church was made necessary by Christ, would refuse to enter it or to remain in it, could not be saved." Even in the Decree on Ecumenism, we find the statement, "It is only through Christ's Catholic Church, which is 'the all-embracing means of salvation,' that they can benefit fully from the means of salvation. We believe that Our Lord entrusted all the blessings of the New Covenant to the apostolic college alone, of which Peter is the head, . . . (*The Sixteen Documents of Vatican II*, pp. 124, 198).

So there you have the self-declared position of the self-contained Church. All of it is utterly alien to both the word and the spirit of the New Testament.

Teresa, every cult and false religious group tries to set itself up as the arbiter between man and God, or as the only true channel by which God may be found and worshiped. The Mormons (Latter Day Saints), Jehovah's Witnesses, and others play the same game. Of course, you can see that if they can get people to accept that major premise, then they can control those people, get those people to support them in various ways, and ride high and handsomely over them. And if they are to be regarded as the mouthpiece or spokesmen for God, and their word is to be taken as authorative, there can be no further argument and they can say virtually what they want without being challenged. In this way they could easily take advantage of people since there would be no way whereby anyone could check up on them, for they are understood to be speaking for God Himself.

All this is one reason why God so constituted things that souls might be free, coming directly to Him without any human agency standing between man and God. A greater reason is that God wants and longs for individual, personal fellowship with each soul. It is very humbling to realize that the infinite God really desires that personal touch with you and me. Let us give it to Him.

The Roman Catholic system has reversed God's order. It says that if you want to get to Christ you must come through the Church, instead of seeing that in order to be rightly in the church you must first come to Christ. It says, come into the Church so that you may be saved; the true way is, be saved by Christ and then come into a visible church.

Carrying on such analogy, the ministers and those serving in the Christian church are not first selected and then empowered by "holy orders" to serve effectually, but they should first manifest spiritual gifts and the call of God, then be set apart for service because they do possess and evidence these things (Acts 6:3; etc.).

The Priesthood, As Such, Dispensed With

Now I have not said much about priests and priesthood, of which Church authorities, as we have seen, say such extravagant things. What about this office in the New Testament?

I took my Greek concordance to the New Testament and checked the word "priest"—Greek, *hiereus*—and I found some interesting, if not amazing, things. It is used only of Jewish priests in reference to the Old Testament order of things, and never once in the singular of any Christian church officer or minister. I say in the singular, because a few times **all believers** are referred to as a "spiritual priesthood" (I Peter 2:5, 9; Apocalypse 1:6; 5:10; 20:6). But never, *never* is any office of priest mentioned in connection with the New Testament church. I would challenge any of your friends to show any place in the New Testament where that term is used of a minister, in the sense of an officiating priest.[1] The only priests known in Scripture were of the tribe of Levi (Hebrews 7:5). They were always married. Their work was in contrast to Christ's great and final work (Hebrews 10:11, 12).

There is no hint of the apostles or other leaders in the New Testament taking over, or directing others to take over, any counterpart of the Levitical priesthood, or of serving in any corresponding place under the new covenant. And why? Let us see.

The book, *Channels of Redemption,* from which I recently quoted, has this to say: "Protestants do not call their clergy priests, because in their religion there is not present that office which is the proper function of the priest, the office of offering real sacrifice to God. The name priest, if used in its proper sense, can be applied only to one who . . . offers a real Sacrifice" (p. 174). Indeed, that is true. But as I have already shown, the one sacrifice for sins was once made, not to be repeated, and there is "no longer offering for sin" (Hebrews 10:18). Therefore there is no sacrificing priest in the New Testament church and no need for any. We should rejoice that we are freed from such, that we have now "a new and living way" (Hebrews 10:20).

Even further, nowhere in the New Testament is the material building or edifice of a church referred to. This may come as a shock to some who depend so completely upon its facilities. Though believers might meet for praise and worship in a house or other sheltered place, the church building was not necessary. Much less

---

[1] Since writing the above I find in that standard authority, *A Catholic Dictionary,* by Addis, Arnold, *et al* (seventeenth edition revised), the unvarnished admission of this in these terms: "The words 'priest,' 'priesthood' (*hiereus, hiereuma*), are never applied in the New Testament to the office of the Christian ministry. . . . The Apostolic Fathers also abstain from any mention of a Christian priesthood" (pp. 675, 676). The last statement quoted clearly gives the lie to the claims of popular Catholic writers such as O'Brien who, in this connection, speak of "the unanimous voice of Christian antiquity. From the earliest days we find express reference in the writings of the Fathers to bishops, priests and deacons . . ." (*The Faith of Millions,* p. 264).

was any material altar needed. There is never reference to an altar in a church. All these things were later developments of men. *(The reference to an altar in Hebrews 13:10 is to the spiritual or heavenly one, in contrast to the one in "the tabernacle" which passed away.)* And, of course, not having an altar we need no priest.

Priests, to be sure, are supposed to stand between men and God in such matters as hearing confession, assessing penance, absolving from sin, and performing rites for the souls of the dead and the living. This they can do, it is thought, because through their consecration by holy orders they stand in a position above the rest of common mortals.

The fact is, however, that all true Christians now not only have direct access to God, as has been pointed out, but also stand on an absolute equality before God. This fact is seen, first, in there being "no respect of persons" with God.

The truth about this is also seen in such places as where Jesus said, in Matthew 23:8-10, "But do not you be called 'Rabbi'; for one is your Master, and all you are brothers. And call no one on earth your father; for one is your Father, who is in heaven. Neither be called masters; for one only is your Master, the Christ." Notice especially that phrase, "and all you are brothers." And observe that these words were not spoken to just the apostles, but (Verse 1), "Jesus spoke to the crowds and to his disciples," which included the apostles and put them, with all the others, on the same level.

Or turn to Luke 9:49, 50, where we read of one of the favorite apostles: "John answered and said, 'Master, we saw a man casting out devils in thy name, and we forbad him, because he does not follow with us.' And Jesus said unto him, 'Do not forbid him; for he who is not against you is for you.'" None needed to follow the apostles or be submissive to them; rather, the right of independent, individual action was readily granted.

A bit further in the same chapter of Luke (Verses 51-56), the apostles asked if they should call down judgment upon a village which did not receive them, but Jesus immediately rebuked such an exclusive spirit.

Again, in Luke 22:24-26, we read, "Now there arose also a dispute among them, which of them was reputed to be the greatest. But he said to them, 'The kings of the Gentiles lord it over them, and they who exercise authority over them are called Benefactors. But not so with you. On the contrary, let him who is greatest among you become as the youngest.'" Thus, contrary to earthly systems with their variously graded ranks, Jesus' followers were to act differently.

All of this certainly speaks for itself. How different it is from that system which places clergy above other believers and makes them arbiters of men's souls!

I might add only that we, as Bible believers, have ministers or pastors in our churches who give themselves fully to their work, but who possess no sacramental powers, who have no inherent right to rule others, and who of themselves bestow no grace to any soul.

How Is God to Be Worshiped?

Now, if Christian believers have no earthly priests, and no altar is needed, and no sanctuary plays any necessary part in the service of God, how then is God to be worshiped?

Holy Scripture reveals this also to us. Observe first the negative side. In Acts 17 we read the account of the Apostle Paul as he spoke to the men of Athens. He said, "I see that in every respect you are extremely religious." Then he referred to their "altar." He came to the point when he declared, "God, who made the world and all that is in it, since he is Lord of heaven and earth, does not dwell in temples built by hands; neither is he served by human hands as though he were in need of anything. . . ." (Verses 22-25). Mark the words; they hardly need comment.

Similarly, in Acts 7, St. Stephen addressed a crowd in Jerusalem, including priests, saying, "Not in houses made by hands does the Most High dwell, even as the prophet says, 'The heaven is my throne, and the earth a footstool for my feet; What house will you build me, says the Lord, or what shall be the place of my resting?'" (Verses 48, 49).

We find very much the same in Hebrews 8:1, 2, and 9:11, statements which are summarized in 9:24 in the words, "For Jesus has not entered into a Holies made with hands," and He, and He alone, is "to appear now before the face of God on our behalf."

Continuing in this book of Hebrews we come to the positive side. In chapter 12:22, 23, we are distinctly told, "But you have come to . . . the heavenly Jerusalem . . . to the Church of the first-born who are enrolled in the heavens." You see, then, how earthly or material things are no longer necessary in the worship of God.

More directly on the positive side, in John 4 Jesus said to a woman who was worshiping in a temple in Samaria, "You worship what you do not know; . . . But the hour is coming, and now is here, when the true worshippers will worship the Father in spirit and in truth. For the Father also seeks such to worship him. God is spirit, and they who worship him must worship in spirit and in truth" (Verses 22-24). You can see the contrast which is brought out.

Observe the contrast again in statements given us by inspiration through the Apostle Paul. He speaks of believers "who serve God in spirit, who glory in Christ Jesus and have no confidence in the flesh" (Philippians 3:3). And, "But now we have been set free from the Law, . . . so that we may serve in newness of spirit and not in oldness of letter" (Romans 7:6). Again, "For whoever are led by the Spirit of God, they are the sons of God. Now you have not received a spirit of bondage so as to be again in fear, but you have received a spirit of adoption as sons, by virtue of which we cry, 'Abba! Father!'" (Romans 8:14, 15). One more, "Seek the things that are above, where Christ is seated at the right hand of God. Mind the things that are above, not the things that are on earth" (Colossians 3:1, 2). These are strong words and can well be pondered.

St. Peter, too, speaks of believers, even those "as newborn

babes" who are built "into a spiritual house," and they are "to offer spiritual sacrifices acceptable to God" (I Peter 2:2, 5). How can anyone miss the significance of all this?

To be sure, we Christians now have buildings in which we gather to worship, but there is nothing about these structures necessary in the approach to God nor for the intrinsic benefit of the soul. Essentially we could worship just as well in an open field, weather and the peace of the surrounding community permitting. Thus we assemble for united prayer, praise and the hearing of the Word of God, and for mutual fellowship in accord with the simplicity inculcated by the New Testament.

You see, instead of having a material building as something necessary today, God has said He would indwell His people and He intends them to be His temple. It is set down in I Corinthians 3, "You are God's tillage, God's building" (Verse 9), and, "Do you not know that you are the temple of God and that the Spirit of God dwells in you? . . . holy is the temple of God, and this temple you are" (Verses 16, 17). This was addressed to the believers at Corinth, and it is put in such a way to show that they should have known it.

Again, to the same group of people: "And what agreement has the temple of God with idols? For you are the temple of the living God, as God says, 'I will dwell and move among them. . . .' " (II Corinthians 6:16). That is the new and higher arrangement of the new covenant, above and higher than that of the old order.

Oh, Teresa, I hope you see how all of this touches our personal relation to God and how free and easy it is to come to Him. Return a moment to the theme begun in this letter, that of the Lord wanting us to come *directly* to Him. **That is the heart of things!**

Ponder thoughtfully Jesus' wonderful, yet simple, invitation in Matthew 11:28, "Come to me, all you who labor and are burdened, and I will give you rest." Of course you see He says, "Come to *Me*," and not to any one or any thing else. And it is, come "all." There is no distinction and no qualification.

Turning to the last book of the Bible, the same Lord Jesus is pleading with us. He says, "Behold, I stand at the door and knock. If any man listens to my voice and opens the door to me, I will come in to him and will sup with him, and he with me" (Apocalypse 3:20). Again it is, **"if any man. . ."** It is for even the *least* of us. And the blessed promise is that if we open the door of our hearts to Him, He *will* come into our lives and "sup," or have wonderful fellowship, with us.

Similarly, in John 14:23, Jesus says, "If anyone love me, he will keep my word, and my Father will love him, and we will come to him and make our abode with him." Don't you long to experience that? You can, and so easily.

In closing, I will remind you of Jesus' parable of the Good Shepherd. The shepherd had ninety-nine safe in the fold. One was out and lost. He longed for that one. The lesson is that the Lord longs with compassion for one insignificant person who is not with Him. Then He does not send someone else after that one, but He Himself goes "after that which is lost, until he finds it" (Luke 15:3-7). What concern; what tenderness! Let us appreciate all of this and respond accordingly.

7

The Source of Spiritual Truth and Its Accessibility to All!

Where the Sincere Soul Can Find Full Light

Dear Teresa:

Our discussion has been getting somewhat extended. Those who have become deeply involved in a closely knit system such as we are considering always seem to have something more to bring up. I have tried to face the major issues and weigh them carefully. That is what you wanted.

If you think, Teresa, that I have put too much emphasis on older points of view, let me assure you that I, too, am aware that a less strict attitude on many of these matters prevails since Vatican II. To be sure, the way some of the clergy these days seem to be giving most of their attention to social change and ecumenical interests, one would think that doctrinal matters are fading into the background—that some of the long standing practices of the Church are now of minor significance. And if these things are of secondary importance, it is easy to see how certain of them can be relaxed (the mass in the vernacular instead of Latin, less fasting before communion, the cup extended in certain cases to the laity—just to mention some smaller examples).

A number of my neighbors here, older Catholics deeply imbued in the traditional, are appalled at the changes coming in. They do not at all like the new trends and wonder if the Church is being weakened.

An Unchanging Church?

But all of this change just goes to show that the Church may not have been so sure of its ground as it thought it was. If it cannot be wrongly led because it alone was founded of God and assured of not being able to err, how does it happen that now it is changing so much?

As an example of how the Church is not supposed to change, in the *Manual of Theology* by P. Geiermann, from which I previously quoted, we read, "The Catholic Church is divine in her guidance. . . . The very nature of a divine Church is that of an infallible guide to man. . . . During the course of the centuries she has never been called on to retract her teaching of faith and morals" (pp. 231, 232). Again, in Kinkead's *An Explanation of the*

Baltimore Catechism (also previously cited), we find, "On matters of faith and morals the Holy Father . . . could not make a mistake in such things. . . . If then the Church could make mistakes in teaching faith and morals, the Holy Ghost could not be with it, and our Lord did not tell the truth" (p. 136). Even Cardinal Gibbons, in his long popular book *The Faith of Our Fathers*, says, "The Church never has and never could have fallen from the truth. . . . If the Catholic Church could preach error, would not God Himself be responsible for the error? And could not the faithful soul say to God with all reverence and truth: Thou hast commanded me, O Lord, to hear Thy Church; if I am deceived by obeying her, Thou art the cause of my error? . . . The Church is not susceptible of being reformed in her doctrines. . . . She will tolerate no doctrinal variations in the future. . . . How much more strictly are not we obliged to be docile to the teachings of the Catholic Church, our Mother . . . whose precepts are immutable" (pp. 55, 56, 57, 61, 62).

If, therefore, some of the things to which I have called attention are now being relegated to the background and the emphasis is being shifted, those in former days who regarded such things as paramount were mistaken. But many of the long-standing distinctives of the Catholic Church were not based on direct scriptural precepts. One contributing factor to their now being relaxed could well be that the Church has become more lenient in allowing the study of the Bible.

We thus see two simultaneous trends in vogue today, even though there is no apparent connection between them. The one is the increased concern with social matters and the world situation. The other is a liberalized attitude in letting the Church's adherents look into things for themselves, even to giving impetus to the study of Scripture. Some visionary folk are wrapped up in the first—social change. But many are more concerned with their own soul's deep needs. They want spiritual peace and assurance. They are very sincere, and if they would only turn diligently to the Word of God they would find the answer to these needs.

Although the Church belatedly allows the reading of the Bible, I have found very few who give much attention to reading it— even the Catholic editions—as it is and for its own sake. This is most unfortunate. They may follow a prayer book or daily missal. They may have on their shelves copies of the Catholic Bible or New Testament, but they do not take the Word of God as it is and read it in order to let it speak directly to them.

Of course many so-called Protestants are not reading their Bibles as they should either. But by and large the leading principles of their faith have been predicated upon its teaching, and the reading of it confirms that this is so, while the more it is read the less it gives substance to Rome's teaching.

The Bible To Be Read By All

Perhaps the reason why more folk do not give much thought to the reading of the Bible itself is because they have been led to believe that it is too hard to understand, or that the interpreting of it should be left to those in the Church who have specialized in such matters and who have been duly appointed to convey to the faithful what they should know. That seems to be an easy way out. But two things may be said here. First, the Church wants the faithful to read the Holy Scriptures. Second, the Bible itself shows that it should be read by all and that it can be understood.

Look first at what the Church says. I may begin with the Pope himself. In some recent editions of the new Catholic Bible there appears a strong statement of Pope Paul VI, given at the Vatican on September 18, 1970, on the importance and value of using the Bible. The highlights are:

> "The holy task of spreading God's Word to the widest possible readership has a special urgency today. . . . In its pages we recognize His voice, we hear a message of deep significance for every one of us. Through the spiritual dynamism and prophetic force of the Bible, the Holy Spirit spreads his light and his warmth over all men, in whatever historical or sociological situation they find themselves.
>
> Paulus P P VI"

Then, in the copy of the New Testament prepared by the Confraternity of Christian Doctrine (1941 edition, St. Anthony Guild Press), from which the many quotations I have heretofore presented are taken, there appears in the front the following statements *"On The Reading Of Holy Scripture"* taken from the Encyclical Letter of Pope Benedict XV (1920). Notice how it includes the whole "human race" and the "laity," and is not just for the clergy but is for all "the faithful."

"The Holy Spirit, the Comforter, had bestowed the Scripture on the human race for their instruction in Divine things . . . and so provide for the faithful plenteous 'consolation afforded by the Scriptures' (Rom. 15, 4) . . .

"We, Venerable Brethren, shall, with St. Jerome as our guide, never desist from urging the faithful to read daily the Gospels, the Acts and the Epistles, so as to gather thence food for their souls . . . We confidently hope that his example will fire both clergy and laity with enthusiasm for the study of the Bible. . . . So convinced indeed was Jerome that familiarity with the Bible was the royal road to the knowledge and love of Christ that he did not hesitate to say: 'Ignorance of the Bible means ignorance of Christ'. . . .

"Our one desire for all the Church's children is that, being saturated with the Bible, they may arrive at the all-surpassing knowledge of Jesus Christ."

I have other editions of the Catholic Bible which present further statements recommending the reading of Scripture (as that from Pope Leo XIII, Pius X, etc.), but let me call attention to more recent declarations from the Decrees of Vatican Council II.

Among one of the first is, "The treasures of the Bible are to be opened up more lavishly, so that richer fare may be provided for the faithful at the table of God's word" (*The Sixteen Documents of Vatican II*, Daughters of St. Paul edition, p. 33).

Then, in the "Dogmatic Constitution On Divine Revelation," we read, "The force and power of the word of God is so great that it stands as the support and energy of the Church, the strength of faith for her sons, the food of the soul, the pure and everlasting source of spiritual life. Consequently these words are perfectly applicable to Sacred Scripture: 'For the word of God is living and active' (Heb. 4:12) and 'it has power to build you up and give you your heritage among all those who are sanctified' (Acts 20:32). Easy access to Sacred Scripture should be provided for all the Christian Faithful" (Ibid., p. 387).

Now see more directly what Scripture itself has to say on this subject. Looking into it carefully we find that it was intended to be read and even studied by all believers. Its persuit was not to be the special privilege alone of the clergy or any other group.

In the seventeenth chapter of Acts we read of how those in a place called Berea were commended for their attention to the Word of God. The record is, "Now these were of a nobler character than those of Thessalonica and they received the word with great eagerness, studying the Scriptures every day to see whether these things were so" (Acts 17:11). You see, the people at large searched the Scriptures, and that daily, to see if what they were told was so. If earnest souls would do that today, there would be less confusion and diversity as to what to believe.

The Old Testament likewise inculcates the searching of Scripture. We read, "Blessed are they that search his testimonies" (Psalm 118:2, Douay; 119 in A.V.). Again, "Search ye diligently in the book of the Lord, and read" (Isaiah 34:16). It truly is "the book of the Lord" which all sincere souls should search.

Turning again to the New Testament, St. Peter, writing to common believers, says, "And we have the word of prophecy, surer still, to which you do well to attend, as to a lamp shining in a dark place" (II Peter 1:19). Let us attend to it, then.

St. Paul addresses his epistle to the Corinthians this way: "To the church of God at Corinth, to . . . all who call upon the name of our Lord Jesus Christ in every place" (I Corinthians 1:2). You see it was for "all" who call upon Christ "in every place." The scope of those who were to be included was not limited.

Again, Paul shows how the epistles were to be passed around and read by all. To the Colossian believers he says, "And when this letter has been read among you, see that it be read in the church of the Laodiceans also; and that you yourselves read the letter from Laodicea" (Colossians 4:16). In fact, we can say that the whole New Testament was so written and so intended.

In Luke 16:19-31, a rich man who landed in Hades wanted someone to go and by personal word warn his five brothers of the dangers of coming to that place. These brothers were not theologians or ecclesiastics, but the answer was that they have "Moses and the Prophets; let them hearken to them."

A couple of quotations from St. John's writings aptly fit in here. He records that Jesus said, "He who is of God hears the words of God. The reason why you do not hear is that you are not of God" (John 8:47). And, "Jesus answered and said, 'If anyone love me, he will keep my word. . . . He who does not love me does not keep my words'" (John 14:23, 24). Notice that the Word is for "anyone" who loves the Lord. Once more, in John's last book we find, "Blessed is he who reads and those who hear the words of this prophecy, and keeps the things that are written therein" (Apocalypse 1:3).

An interesting and significant thing occurred in an incident recorded in Luke 11:27, 28. After Jesus had been teaching, "a certain woman lifted up her voice from the crowd, and said to him, 'Blessed is the womb that bore thee'." In other words she said, "Blessed be the Virgin Mary." But Jesus quickly replied, "Rather, blessed are they who hear the word of God and keep it." Think that through.

Is The Bible Too Hard To Understand?

Now, what about those who regard the Bible with a sense of awe but who have been led to believe that it is too hard to understand and who honestly feel they are not capable of interpreting it properly? Well, the Book has its own answer to that. It shows that it can be understood, and even by the young.

The Apostle Paul, writing to Timothy, reminds him that "from thy infancy thou hast known the Sacred Writings [*the holy scriptures*—Douay], which are able to instruct thee unto salvation by the faith which is in Christ Jesus. All Scripture is inspired by God and useful for teaching, for reproving, for correcting, for instructing in justice" (II Timothy 3:15, 16, Confraternity).

In Matthew 11:25, Jesus said, "I praise thee, Father, Lord of heaven and earth, that thou didst hide these things from the wise and prudent, and didst reveal them to little ones." Both of those passages show that even children can gain what is needed from Scripture; surely, then, adults can profit from it even more.

The same essential truth is found in the Old Testament. Take the longest chapter in the Bible, Psalm 119 (or, as it is in the Douay version, Psalm 118). It contains 176 verses, and virtually every one extolls the Word of God. Synonyms are used for the Scripture, such as the Law of the Lord, or His testimonies, or His commandments, ordinances, precepts, decrees, judgments and so on. But all these refer to the Word of God. They, too, show how even the young should give heed to it and can understand it.

For example (and I quote from the Douay Old Testament), it says, "Thy testimonies are wonderful: therefore my soul hath sought them. The declaration of thy words giveth light: and giveth understanding to little ones" (Verses 129, 130). Again, "I have understood more than all my teachers: because thy testimonies are my meditation. I have had understanding above ancients [elders]: because I have sought thy commandments" (Verses 99, 100). It is really something when you can surpass even learned teachers simply because attention is given to the Word, which itself imparts understanding.

Here is another citation from that magnificent Psalm. The inspired Word says, "Then I shall not be confounded, when I shall look into all thy commandments" (Verse 6). Thus no one need fear that he will be confounded or confused by reading the Bible for himself. It is its own best interpreter.

An earlier Psalm similarly shows the effectiveness of the Word.

69

"The testimony of the Lord is faithful, giving wisdom to little ones . . . . The commandment of the Lord is lightsome, enlightening the eyes" (Psalm 18:8, 9; Psalm 19 in A. V.).

This does not mean that by one reading you can understand every single thing in the Bible. There are many deep things there; but anyone who is sincere and diligent can understand enough to see the great truths of salvation and the Christian faith. The more one studies it, the more he finds that it becomes clear, and it blesses and thrills his soul.

Also we have already seen that the Holy Spirit is given to all true children of God, and that He is specifically indicated as the means of enlightening the Word to those who yield to and obey Him (Ephesians 1:17-19; I John 2:20, 27; etc.).

"Private Interpretation" and the Use of Tradition

There is another thing, Teresa, that I find a number of my Catholic friends stumble over. They have been given to understand that "private interpretation" is condemned; therefore these good folk give little heed to Scripture, thinking that their study of it would involve them in "private interpretation."

That thought is based on words found in II Peter 1:20. But notice the exact wording: "No prophecy of Scripture is made by private interpretation" (both Confraternity and Douay). It is talking about how the prophetic word was *made,* not how it is to be read. You see, the very next words continue, "For not by the will of man was prophecy brought . . ." (Verse 21). That explains it. Scripture is not *the result of* private interpretation on the part of those who wrote it. That is, the men of God through whom it came were not giving their own—their private—ideas, but rather were setting it forth "as they were moved by the Holy Spirit" (same 21st verse).

As to the reading of it, I already quoted the very words of Peter preceding this statement, where he said that we "do well to attend" to this "word of prophecy" (Verse 19). So you see how utterly mistaken is the use of that phrase to discourage study of the Scripture, when actually the import of the whole passage is just the opposite—to show the importance of our attending to it.

A similar example of things being turned right around is the appeal to tradition. The words of Paul to the Thessalonians to "hold the traditions which you have learned" (Douay, II Thessalonians 2:14), is rightly changed in the Confraternity to "hold the teachings that you have learned" (II Thessalonians 2:15). The word "tradition" is corrected to read "teaching." Of course, while the New Testament was being written, believers were taught by word of mouth, but oral teaching was in perfect accord with what was then being recorded in Scripture. Now, since we have the complete New Testament, Scripture is all that we need as our source of instruction, and tradition is actually condemned.

See how Jesus rebuked the following of tradition. We read, "The Pharisees and Scribes asked him, 'Why do not thy disciples walk according to the tradition of the ancients. . . ?' But answering he said to them, 'Well did Isaias prophesy of you hypocrites, as it is written, "This people honors me with their lips, but their heart is

70

far from me; But in vain do they worship me, teaching for doctrines precepts of men." For, letting go the commandment of God, you hold fast the tradition of men. . . .' And he said to them, 'Well do you nullify the commandment of God, that you may keep your own tradition!' " Then Jesus added, "You make void the commandment of God by your tradition, which you have handed down" (Mark 7:5-9, 13; The same is in Matthew 15:1-10). Jesus thus condemned tradition, and neither He nor the apostles ever once appealed to it as authority.

An example of the unreliability of tradition is seen in the record of John 21. Jesus had told Peter that John would outlive him, or not meet such an untimely death as would Peter. "This saying therefore went abroad among the brethren, that that disciple was not to die. But Jesus had not said to him, 'He is not to die'; but rather, 'If I wish him to remain until I come, what is it to thee?' " (John 21:23). Therefore that tradition, or the saying that went abroad among the brethren, was entirely wrong and falsehood was being passed around by tradition.

Here is another reference to tradition. Paul, who before his conversion had shown great zeal "for the traditions of my fathers" (Galatians 1:14), warns against tradition this way: "See to it that no one deceives you by philosophy and vain deceit, according to human traditions, according to the elements of the world and not according to Christ" (Colossians 2:8).

Notice the difference between Scripture and tradition. Tradition is elusive, vague, nebulous. Scripture is manifest by definite delineation. Tradition seems to have no limits. It has such ramifications and is so exhaustless that almost anything can be "proven" by one tradition or another.

Moreover, one tradition can be—*and frequently is*—put in conflict with another. We saw this in considering the wide range of interpretations given to Peter's confession in Matthew sixteen.

The Church's appeal to and dependence on tradition is actually a confession that Catholic beliefs cannot be established by Scripture itself. Something else must be resorted to in the attempt to buoy up the Church's claims. This is a sad acknowledgement.

The biblical condemnation of sources outside of Scripture which we have noted would apply with equal force to the varying pronouncements of church councils and papal edicts. These latter things change or fluctuate, but it appears that God has seen fit to lay before us a stable and unchanging source of truth. Otherwise we could never have any settled assurance of where the truth is. In that long Psalm which extolls the Word of God, we read, "For ever, O Lord, thy word standeth firm in heaven: Thy truth unto all generations" (Douay, Psalm 118:89, 90a; A.V., 119). Or, as the Church's new translation of the Old Testament has it, "Your word, O Lord, endures forever; it is firm as the heavens. Through all generations your truth endures." Again, this new version puts it in the same Psalm: "You, O Lord, are near, and all your commands are permanent. Of old I know from your decrees, that you have established them forever" (Verses 151, 152). Thus we should go to the Word of God as a *final* authority. It is something "permanent," not shifting or subject to human adjustment—no matter how great that human instrument may seem to be.

Similar is the thought expressed in this new version in Psalm 111: "Sure are all his precepts, reliable forever and ever, wrought in truth and equity" (Verses 7b, 8).

It is not surprising then that we read this injunction in Isaiah 8:20 (Douay), "To the law rather, and to the testimony. And if they speak not according to this word, they shall not have the morning light." We are to base religious teaching "according to this word," that is, according to the Scripture.

St. Peter, too, quotes from Isaiah, "The word of the Lord endures forever" (I Peter 1:25). Nothing else has such guarantees behind it.

St. Jude exhorts us to hold to "the faith once for all delivered to the saints" (Jude 3). If the true faith was "once for all" delivered, nothing more is needed.

The Bible closes with this fearsome warning: "I testify to everyone who hears the words of the prophecy of this book. If anyone shall add to them, God will add unto him the plagues that are written in this book" (Apocalypse 22:18).

St. Paul, therefore, can say, "We at least, are not, as many others, adulterating the word of God" (II Corinthians 2:17). Let us, too, not turn to anything which would add to or adulterate the holy Scriptures.

Now I think, Teresa, that this answers the point as to why I have been basing everything so much on Scripture. You say that I keep quoting the Bible here and quoting it there. Yes, indeed, and now you see the reason for this. God intended it to be our unfailing source of truth and a sure spiritual light.

Jesus revealed the source of error when He said, "You err because you know neither the Scriptures nor the power of God" (Matthew 22:29). And in His parable of the sower He said, "The seed is the word of God. . . . That upon good ground, these are they who, with a right and good heart, having heard the word, hold it fast, and bear fruit in patience" (Luke 8:11, 15).

Finally, St. Paul, writing to all the believers at Rome, says, "For whatever things have been written have been written for our instruction, that through the patience and consolation afforded by the Scriptures we may have hope" (Romans 15:4). Therefore the question we should ask is the one with which Paul challenged the Romans: "What does the Scripture say?" (Romans 4:3; also the Galatians—Galatians 4:30).

We all, therefore, need to recognize the Bible as our sole source of authority in religious matters, and we need to go to it for ourselves to find the truth essential to our spiritual well-being. That, as we have seen, is what God gave it for. Let us then act upon it and earnestly take heed to its infallible precepts.

8

Salvation Assured and Its Groundwork In Grace

Can One Be Certain of His Destiny? On What Basis?

Dear Teresa:

Thank you for your rather brief note. I see that you don't have much to say as far as the main subject matter of our discussion goes. I hope this silence does not indicate that you are wanting to avoid these vital issues. I take it rather that you just don't know what to say. You were quite recently very much taken up with all this. I only hope that your interest may come to rest on solid ground.

Let us go right to the heart of things. Salvation—*one's eternal destiny*—is the most important subject that can be pondered. I know you have been concerned about that.

Salvation and Fullness of Assurance

Having settled the matter of where the source of all truth lies—the Scripture—and finding that this wellspring of instruction is accessible to all, we may now turn to it to see how the soul's deep needs may be met. How wonderful that God has not left us in the dark, but has shown clearly how we may have full assurance of salvation—and that, right here and now!

Those strictly adhering to the Church, however, are left without any confidence that they may die in a "state of grace." One is made very conscious of his sin and unworthiness. And he is conditioned to be very dependent upon the instrumentality of the Church. But he never feels sure of anything sufficient to warrant his claiming assurance of his soul's highest welfare. He does not know just how things may work out for his spiritual destiny. He would not dare to assume that his salvation is now settled. In fact, the Catechism says, "If a man thinks his salvation already secure he sins by presumption" (*The Catechism Explained*, Spirago-Clarke, p. 280). That is a tragic concept. That is just what a God of love who has genuine concern for His creatures does *not* want them to be left with.

In the Church's teaching there may be found expressions suggesting such things as the efficacy of Christ's death, the value of faith, the desirability of new life imparted by God, and so on. But the manner in which the benefit of these is realized by the individual becomes beclouded by the interposition of sacerdotal functions, rites and ceremonies, human efforts and so forth, all of which eclipse what otherwise might assure the soul.

However, for those who really want to find deliverance from the fear of death, who long to know complete cleansing from all sin, who desire knowledge of immediate acceptance by God and an entrance into Heaven, the Bible has the answer, clear and positive. Many stumble over the simplicity of it all.

Observe, therefore, that we **can** have both *full* and *present* **assurance** of salvation. We don't have to wait through a period of future accounting for sins or until the judgment day. First John 4:17 says, "In this is love perfected with us, that we may have confidence in the day of judgment." And Jesus said, "He who hears my word, and believes him who sent me, has life everlasting, and does not come to judgment, but has passed from death to life" (John 5:24).

To make the force of this great truth stand out, I will cite some leading passages of Scripture and place in bold or emphatic form key words which emphasize the vital elements. (All quotations taken, as usual, from the Confraternity New Testament, 1946.)

Turning in the chapter in I John following the one from which I just quoted, we read, "These things I am writing to you that you may **KNOW** that you have eternal life—you who believe in the name of the Son of God" (I John 5:13). Then, a few verses following, we find that strong word "know" three times: "We **KNOW** that we are of God. . . . And we **KNOW** that the Son of God has come and has given us understanding, that we may **KNOW** the true God and may be in his true Son" (I John 5:19, 20). That is positive; that gives assurance. And all true believers are included in the "we" who may know. Again, in I John 3:14 is the simple, declarative statement, "We **KNOW** that we have passed from death to life." And notice the tense of the verb "have passed." It shows that it is accomplished, and may therefore be presently realized.

In II Timothy 1:12 we read, "For I **KNOW** whom I have believed, and am **CERTAIN** that he is able to guard the trust committed to me against that day." That is the spirit with which the New Testament is permeated: that of **CERTAINTY**, not holding one off with vagaries.

Thinking of death and what follows, we read in II Corinthians 5:1, "For we **KNOW** that if the earthly house in which we dwell [our bodies] be destroyed, we have a building from God, a house not made by human hands, eternal in the heavens." What a glorious hope and how sure believers may be of it!

If, as it was said of John the Baptist, he would "give to his people knowledge of salvation through forgiveness of their sins" (Luke 1:77), how much would the Lord Jesus Christ give that to His people!

A Salvation Presently Possessed

Look at some passages which show that all of this is for us right now. Going back to I John, we find, "Beloved, **NOW** we are the children of God" (I John 3:2). Having looked at II Corinthians

5, we may note in the next chapter, "Behold, **NOW** is the acceptable time; behold, **NOW** is the day of salvation!" (II Corinthians 6:2). This is something we should rejoice in; indeed, "we exult also in God through our Lord Jesus Christ, through whom we have **NOW** received reconciliation" (Romans 5:11). And, of course, the tense of "having now received" shows that we have it in the present, not something we merely hope for in the future. The first verse of the same chapter says, **"HAVING BEEN** justified therefore by faith, let us have peace with God."

We often refer to our already being saved as a present-tense-salvation. The Word of God abundantly confirms this. For example, Colossians 1:13, 14, says, "He has rescued us from the power of darkness and transferred us into the kingdom of his beloved Son, in whom we have received our redemption, the remission of our sins." You see, it is conveyed in "has rescued us" and "transferred," and "we have received" our redemption. Then, in the next chapter, we read, "In him [Christ] dwells all the fullness of the Godhead bodily, and in him who is the head of every Principality and Power you **HAVE RECEIVED** of that fullness." And, "When you were dead by reason of your sins . . . he brought to life, forgiving you **ALL** your sins, cancelling the decree against us, which was hostile to us. Indeed, he **HAS TAKEN** it **COMPLETELY** away, nailing it to the cross" (Colossians 2:9, 10, 13, 14).

Similarly, in Ephesians it is stated, "he . . . brought us to life together with Christ—by grace you **HAVE BEEN** saved. . . . For by grace you **HAVE BEEN** saved through faith" (Ephesians 2:5, 8). Again, in the next chapter, ". . . Christ Jesus our Lord. In him we have **ASSURANCE** and **CONFIDENT** access through faith in him" (Ephesians 3:12). And in the following chapter, ". . . as also God in Christ **HAS** generously **FORGIVEN** you" (Ephesians 4:32).

To the believers in Corinth, Paul wrote, "For the doctrine of the cross is . . . to those who **ARE SAVED,** that is, to us, it is the power of God" (I Corinthians 1:18). And Paul, who said this, seemed not in the least to be afraid of committing the "sin of presumption."

To those in Rome, Paul said, "The Spirit himself gives testimony to our spirit that **WE ARE** sons of God" (Romans 8:16).

St. John puts it this way: "I am writing to you, dear children, because your sins **ARE FORGIVEN** you for his name's sake" (I John 2:12).

The same writer, as we saw, records Jesus saying, "He who hears my word, and believes him who sent me, **HAS** life everlasting and does not come to judgment, but **HAS PASSED** from death to life" (John 5:24).

I could go on and quote passage after passage which speaks of our already having eternal life, or, of our being right now children of God, our being cleansed or forgiven of all sin, our already being assured of a place in Heaven and having a glorious inheritance. Read the New Testament for yourself and you will see that it fairly breathes with this sense of the believer already possessing what God provides for His own, and what Christ came to make possible while we are still on this earth.

Why Man's Works Do Not Avail With God

You noticed, no doubt, that some of those texts just quoted refer to faith as the means by which this full salvation is received. This also could be brought out again and again—faith being designated as the sufficient and only means whereby one becomes saved. Now, of course, all Catholics will say that their faith is in Christ as much (or more) than anyone else's. But in fact, they *also* believe that in order to get the full benefits of the gospel, they further must observe the sacraments, do penance, perform good works, be faithful in prayers, gain merit, and so on. They would resist the idea of *faith only* being the means of salvation.

Many persons feel that receiving everything by faith alone would be too easy, or that surely man has to make some effort, or pay some price, or offer God something in order to receive His salvation. However, God loves us so much that He wanted to do it all Himself so that our gratitude and thanks would be to Him alone. Would not a loving earthly father, who really cares for his young son and who has abundant resources, want to provide the very best benefits for that son as a token of his love and concern? And he would not expect that child to laboriously struggle in making payment for the boon extended, would he?

God's love toward man is infinite (Jeremiah 31:3). He went to the utmost in providing Christ (Romans 8:32) and allowing Him to suffer so great a death (Philippians 2:8) whereby the penalty of sin was fully paid (Colossians 2:13, 14). As a result, God will provide *everything* for our salvation or *nothing*. It is all in what God has done for man, not at all in what man does for God. We come to receive, not with something in our hands, but empty handed. In this way it may be seen that "the abundance of the power is God's and not ours" (II Corinthians 4:7).

When you stop to think about it, God is so great that He does not need anything from us. As we saw in Acts 17, He is not "served by human hands as though he were in need of anything" (Acts 17:25). Or, as God said to Job, "Who hath given me before that I should repay him? All things that are under heaven are mine" (Job 41:2, Douay; 41:11 in A.V.).

When offerings have fulfilled their mission or become perfunctory, we read, "I have no pleasure in you, saith the Lord of hosts: and I will not receive a gift at your hand" (Malachias 1:10). And in the book of Amos the Lord goes so far as to say, "I hate and have rejected your festivities: and I will not receive the odour of your assemblies. And if you offer me holocausts and your gifts, I will not receive them" (Amos 6:21, 22). This is reiterated in the New Testament (e.g., Hebrews 10:5, 6).

On the other hand, the Lord shows that He, and He alone, wants to be recognized as the source of all spiritual good. In Isaiah He says, "For my own sake, for my own sake, will I do it, that I may not be blasphemed: and I will not give my glory to another"; and, again, "I, the Lord: that is my name. I will not give my glory to another, nor my praise to graven things" (Isaiah 48:11; 42:8). God recognizes such a prayer as we find in the

Psalms, "Help us, O God, our saviour; and for the glory of thy name, O Lord, deliver us: and forgive us our sins for thy name's sake" (Psalm 78:9; 79:9 in A.V.). Probably many people pray prayers like that without stopping to realize just what is indicated. If it is for His sake alone, then it is not because of anything that we may lay claim to. As stated in Isaiah again, "I am, I am he that blot out thy iniquities for my own sake: and I will not remember thy sins" (Isaiah 43:25).

Although there was a place for sacrifices for a time, they merely pointed to Christ, finding their fulfillment in Him when He became the "mediator of a superior covenant," or when He provided "a new and living way" (Hebrews 8:6; 10:20). Now such doings are regarded as dead forms. Therefore it is declared, "How much more will the blood of Christ . . . cleanse your conscience from dead works" (Hebrews 9:14). The Apostle Paul censured those depending upon ceremonies and observances by saying, "How is it that you turn again to the weak and beggarly elements, which you desire to serve again? You are observing days and months and seasons and years. I fear for you, lest perhaps I have labored among you in vain" (Galatians 4:9-11). Instead, we are those who now "serve God in spirit, who glory in Christ Jesus and have no confidence in the flesh" (Philippians 3:3).

For such reasons, God has placed faith as the only means of our becoming beneficiaries of what He has provided.

Faith An Exclusive Means

Note how faith is set off as the antithesis of works, and not that works is an equal or co-essential in procuring salvation. We read in Ephesians 2:8, 9: "For by grace you have been saved through faith; and that not from yourselves, for it is the gift of God; not as the outcome of works." That is clear and unqualified, and that is the Word of God. Again, "But when the goodness and kindness of God our Saviour appeared, then not by reason of good works that we did ourselves, but according to his mercy he saved us" (Titus 3:4, 5).

Abraham's faith is set forth as the standard, even for us. We read in the New Testament, "For what does the Scripture say? 'Abraham believed God and it was credited to him for justice.' Now to him who works, the reward is not credited as a favor but as something due. But to him who does not work, but believes in him who justifies the impious, his faith is credited to him as justice" (Romans 4:3-5). Then, later in the same chapter, it is added that it "was the outcome of faith, that it might be a favor, in order that it might be secure for . . . those who are of the faith of Abraham"; and, "Now not for his sake only was it written that 'It was credited to him,' but for the sake of us also, to whom it will be credited if we believe" (Verses 16, 23, 24). Thus Abraham is our pattern; we are to be saved the same way that he was. Abraham stood justified, but *not* on the grounds of any works or deeds that he did. Abraham was not saved because he kept the ten commandments; they were given long after his day. He was not saved by faithfulness to a church, there was none then in existence. Baptism was wholly unknown to him. The Old Testament rituals and religious ceremonies were brought in much later under the Levitical system. (Abraham was declared justified before circumcision was introduced.) Yet Abraham was saved, and we are told that we are saved in the same way; that is, by faith.

We also find it stated in Romans, "For by works of the law no human being shall be justified before him," and, "For we reckon that a man is justified by faith independently of the works of the Law" (Romans 3:20, 28).

Very much the same is found in Galatians 2:16, "But we know that a man is not justified by the works of the Law, but by the faith of Jesus Christ. Hence we also believe in Christ Jesus, that we may be justified by the faith of Christ, and not by the works of the Law; because by the works of the Law no man will be justified." You see in all of these statements how faith and works are contrasted or set off the one from the other. And it is faith that saves!

Faith or belief being the instrument of our salvation is made plain in such statements as that in Acts, where it says of certain ones who came to "hear the word of the gospel and believe," God then "cleansed their hearts by faith" (Acts 15:7-9). Also we read of those "who have faith to the saving of the soul" (Hebrews 10:39), and of those who "believe in him for the attainment of life everlasting" (I Timothy 1:16). Again in Romans it says that the gospel "is the power of God unto salvation to every one who believes" (Romans 1:16). Still further we find that "It pleased God . . . to save those who believe" (I Corinthians 1:21). And, "All who believe in him may receive forgiveness of sins" (Acts 10:43). The declaration of Jesus, "Those who believe in him may not perish, but may have everlasting life," is repeated twice in John 3 (Verses 15, 16), while the same chapter closes with the words, "He who believes in the Son has everlasting life" (Verse 36). In none of these statements is works associated with salvation; in fact, it would nullify them if works were a requirement.

The phrase sometimes quoted, "Work out your own salvation," is wholly misapplied, for where it appears there is immediately added that "it is God . . . who works in you" (Philippians 2:12, 13). That refers to the out-working or manifesting of a salvation already possessed.

Works is discounted in John 6 as the thing which makes one acceptable to God. There we find that certain zealous people put the question directly to Jesus, "What are we to do in order that we may perform the works of God? In answer Jesus said to them, 'This is the work of God, that you believe in him whom he has sent' " (John 6:28, 29). This "believe" is the only ground of acceptance with God.

Faith And Works Properly Related

Now I am quite aware that some will at once say something like this: *a man can say that he believes and then live any kind of a life, no matter how bad, and he will be saved—is that right?* This is a popular misconception over which many stumble.

To advocate works as a means of salvation is to confuse the **fruits** of being saved with its **roots.** Good works is the outcome, not the source. True faith, the root, manifests itself in righteous living. Thus, the faith of a man who says, "I will believe and then live as I please," is no faith at all. Anyone who professes to have faith in Christ and still lives an evil life, may be both deceived and attempting to deceive others.

When a man truly believes—**believes in his heart**—he will want to do right, will want to live a good life. Long observation has abundantly borne this out. The explanation of it is seen in several important considerations:

First, upon true heart belief in the Savior, a man is born again and receives a new nature (John 1:12, 13; James 1:18; I Peter 1:23; II Peter 1:4). Study these verses of Scripture and you will see this wonderful truth. Sacramentarian rites have nothing to do with it. The new nature within a Christian impels to good works. A man may need to be urged to yield to this new nature and let it grow, but as he submits to it after he is saved, there will be a real difference in his life.

Secondly, as brought out earlier, when one becomes a child of God, the Holy Spirit comes to make His abode with that one and, unless he resists, will lead that one on in the Christian life and in good works. If he does resist, the Holy Spirit will make him feel very uncomfortable and he may even be chastened for his lack of submission (Hebrews 12:5-13). This chastening is exercised on certain ones because they are already sons of God, not in order that they may become sons of God.

Thirdly, if one truly accepts the Savior, it means he believes that Christ actually suffered and died for his sins, taking upon Himself the penalty of all his iniquity, paying such a great price for his redemption that, out of gratitude and appreciation, he will want to "do those things that are pleasing in his sight" (Hebrews 13:21; I John 3:22). If a man professes to love Christ and disobeys His commandments, it shows that his profession is a farce (I John 2:3-5).

Fourthly, as the new believer studies his Bible he will come to see that good works do not bring one salvation, but that the Lord does reward those who are His children for their good deeds and service (Mattheww 10:41, 42; 16:27; Luke 14:12-14; I Corinthians 3:8, 14; Colossians 3:22-24; Hebrews 10: 35, 36; II John 8; Apocalypse 22:12). Being saved by faith and receiving rewards for service are two very different things. This needs to be understood.

You see, a believer should be encouraged in Christian conduct by the fact that he already is saved, rather than assuming that by trying to imitate Christian conduct he may become saved. Working and striving, accompanied by a sense of uncertainty, never yield the cheerfulness, confidence and hearty obedience to God which springs from a sense of forgiveness, reconciliation and sonship.

Bible salvation, which includes full cleansing from sin, is by faith alone. All other religions are systems of works. You know, Teresa, that I have taught Comparative Religions for years in several colleges. I have observed that all human religions try to offer God something, accumulate merit, pay a price for deliverance, or gain favor with a deity. Basically there are only two religions. **One is of works**—man's religion. **The other is of faith**—God's way. One cries do, *do* **do**. The other proclaims it is done, *done*, **all done**. The first says man must do; the second says it has all been done for him by the God of love. The first says we must pay for our sins as best we can. The second says it was all paid for on Calvary.

Yes, all false religions are systems of works; they all want to offer God something that they have devised, the only difference being what it is they bring or offer. In God's plan, one just accepts what has been done for him and all credit goes to the great Benefactor. But no heathen religion ever developed such a concept. They only know tedious works and human effort. However, man at his best can never do enough to pay the penalty for his sin which has offended a holy God. Any plan whereby one must do good works, recite various formulas, put trust in sacraments, and so on, is in a class with the heathen religions.

The doctrine of merit appeals to fallen man's vanity; he likes to think of himself as good enough, or able enough to pay at least in part for his salvation. God has revealed, on the contrary, that we must recognize ourselves as quite lost, undone and helpless. Romans 5:6 says, "At the appointed time, when we were still powerless, Christ died for us godless men" (New Confraternity of 1970). Free grace, moreover, cuts right across the natural vanity of the human heart. It is an offense to the tendency in man to be satisfied with himself. It is a stumbling block to man's innate feeling that he can do something or offer God something for his own salvation.

I trust you see, of course, that all of this doesn't mean that good works has no place in the life of a child of God. There is much in Scripture about righteous living and doing good works. But all that is addressed to those who have already become saved, to those who have first received Christ, never as a means of initial acceptance with God. The order here is very important: first receive the Savior wholly apart from your works, then obey the Savior in doing good works solely out of love for Him and to glorify Him. An old cuplet has put it this way:

> *I cannot work my soul to save,*
> *That work the Lord has done;*
> *But I will work like any slave*
> *For love of God's dear Son.*

The Grace of God In Salvation

Now let us go back and relate the matter of being saved by faith alone to the matter of the grace of God. The grace of God—

as far as the saving of a lost soul is concerned—refers to God doing the whole thing and bestowing upon the unworthy that which is undeserved and unmerited. It has been said that grace is everything for nothing to those who don't deserve anything. Grace is the fullness of divine favor without it ever being recompensed for in any way.

Scripture shows that if works enters in anywhere, then that which is received is not of grace. Yet God said that salvation would be by grace. "By grace you have been saved" (Ephesians 2:8, et al). But if works contribute, then grace ceases to be grace, for God says of His saving us, "if out of grace, then not in virtue of works; otherwise grace is no longer grace" (Romans 11:6). Grace is no longer grace if it is granted on the basis of merit having at all prompted its bestowment. Even further, grace would cease to be grace if God withheld it because of unworthiness or ill-desert on the part of the recipient. The undeserving are the very ones for whom grace is intended. If human merit enters the picture, grace must bow out. In other words, it is **all** of grace or it is **not at all** of grace.

Man may *confuse* works and grace, but he can never *fuse* them. They never mix. When the attempt is made to combine them, each loses its own distinctiveness and ceases to be what its name indicates. Works demand something to be done; grace presents something already done. To that extent they are opposites. Instead of making demands and setting forth requirements, grace bestows everything and freely confers boundless blessings on its undeserving objects. Grace is without regard to merit on the side of the recipient, without measure on the part of the great Bestower.

Looking again at the epistle to the Romans, this truth is further brought out when we read, "Now to him that worketh, the reward is not reckoned according to grace but according to debt" (Romans 4:4, Douay). Here it is shown that grace and debt are set off the one from the other. If a thing is worked for, then the one to whom the work is rendered is under debt to pay it. But God will be in debt to no man. If God owed man anything, then that would put Him under obligation to man (something contrary to His exalted nature) and the grant would not be of grace. It would be a matter of bookkeeping: *there would be a debit side and a credit side.* If a man could pay what he thought was lacking or purchase his standing by good works, he could demand the salvation he deems he is entitled to and God would be obligated to give it to him. That is just what the Bible says God will *not* do. "To him that worketh, the reward is not reckoned according to grace but according to debt. But to him that worketh not . . . his faith is reputed to justice, according to the purpose of the grace of God" (Romans 4:4, 5, Douay).

Further, we are told, "Therefore it is of faith, that according to grace the promise might be firm to all" (Romans 4:16, Douay). Also, in the next chapter of Romans, we read, "Grace is from many offenses unto justification. . . . Where the offense has abounded, grace has abounded yet more" (Romans 5:16, 20, Confraternity). In other words, grace is sufficient to more than cover all man's sins and shortcomings.

The deep meaning of grace cannot be too strongly emphasized. Grace is God's saving goodness extended not only to the undeserving and unworthy, but further, to those who of themselves deserve just the opposite—deserve judgment and damnation or to those who not only had no good to offer, but who were transgressors and rightful objects of the wrath of God. And that included all of us.

To bring out what grace is, note this distinction. Love may flow forth in any direction. It may ascend to those above it, reach out to those on a common level, or it may descend to those below it. But grace has only one direction that it can take—it flows downward, it condescends to those beneath it, to those who have no claim upon it and who could never make themselves worthy of it or repay it.

Mercy likewise descends to those in need, but sparing them from the ill due them, leaves them on that lower level. Grace does more. Grace brings its objects up from the depths of misery and woe to a pinnacle of favor as though they had never sinned or fallen short in any way. This is possible in virtue of the standing imparted to them—the perfect standing of that One who never sinned, but who died for their sin. They did not deserve or merit such favor—*quite the opposite*—it is bestowed upon them by pure grace. Grace thus goes far beyond mercy. Mercy takes the bitter cup of penalty and suffering from the hand of the guilty and empties it; grace fills it to the brim with salvation and untold blessings.

Showing the exclusiveness of grace, the epistle to the Galatians says that if a man is justified by anything else he is not in grace. "You who would be justified in the law are estranged from Christ; you have fallen away from grace" (Galatians 5:4). Works is a ladder which we imperfectly construct and painfully endeavor to ascend; grace is a shaft of sunlight bursting forth from the very throne of God and searching us out in no matter how dark and dismal a pit of human misery we may have sunk and lifting us to a plane where the rich blessings of God are showered upon us.

Think of the tragedy of all this. When one seeks salvation by works he can never know when he has worked enough, or repented enough, or prayed enough, or attained enough, or offered enough, or done enough, or obeyed enough, or identified with ceremonies enough, or accumulated merit enough to gain that salvation. **How much better just to accept the full and free saving work of Christ provided through God's infinite grace!**

If man's acceptance with God was of works no one could attain it, for none could accomplish either the quality or quantity of good works necessary to satisfy the just demands of a holy God, or to bridge the gulf between man and God. Accordingly, if salvation is of works, none could be saved; but if it be of grace, no believer need fear being lost, for grace reaches the lowest depths and then transports by its own inherent character to the greatest height.

While we could never achieve grace, the God of infinite love could never fail to grant it. We often fail in our intended faithfulness to God, but He can never fail in His faithfulness to us. That is, we may well doubt our faithfulness to God, but we can never doubt His exhaustless faithfulness to us.

Some people have thought of grace as God giving us the chance to work for our salvation, or as supernatural help in our struggle to gain favor with Him. They might even say it is grace that we can do penance which He accepts, or that we attain grace through the sacraments, and so on. But all of this misses the very heart of grace as we have seen it revealed in Scripture. When the old Baltimore Catechism says, "without grace we can do nothing to *merit* heaven," (Question 111, Kinkead edition, p. 123), it utterly confuses things. Rather, Heaven is all in the merits of Christ.

Sometimes there are other uses of the term grace, as when a Christian may display certain "graces"—*kindliness and friendliness to others*—but grace in that sense should not be identified with the grace of God in relation to the soul's basic needs. Paul may say that grace is given to serve God or help one's fellow men. But that, too, is something else. Neither one's earnestness nor his striving can pay the debt of sin. If it did, salvation would not be of grace. Thus, no one achieves *a state* of grace, for grace is never "achieved." If it were, it wouldn't be grace! Therefore we are "justified *freely* by his grace" (Romans 3:24).

Having emphasized that grace is granted to man wholly apart from any merit or worthiness in him, the question may be asked, **how then does God determine who is to benefit from it?** Does He automatically bestow it upon every man and save the whole human race without distinction (since none deserves it)?

The answer has already been intimated in the place we saw given to faith. A willingness to believe God and accept His gift is the key to its reception. The benefit of God's grace is available to all. In grace, God provided the Savior for the whole world. But He does not force that benefaction upon any man. He merely says that no matter how great a sinner (that is, how undeserving) a man may be, he may be the recipient of that grace by simple faith.

A study of the third through the fifth chapters of Romans will bring all this out very clearly. (Some modern translations render the original word for grace—*charis*—as "favor," but it is the undeserved divine favor, that is, grace, which is meant.) And faith is prominently indicated as the key to it. "Justified freely by his grace . . . through faith" (Romans 3:24, 25, Douay and Confraternity). "It is of faith, that according to grace the promise might be firm to all" (Romans 4:16, Douay). "We also have access by faith into that grace" (Romans 5:2, Douay and Confraternity).

These statements, along with the basic meaning of grace, show why salvation is by faith only. Since not of works, there would be no other way of embracing it except by faith. Grace is the ocean of God's superabundant provision; faith is the cup by which we poor mortals dip up of that soul-satisfying water of life.

God put salvation on the basis of faith so that man would see his own helplessness, trust only in God, and give all the glory to Him. Furthermore, the faith basis makes it entirely fair to everyone. The poor, the weak, the helpless—all have an equal opportunity to be saved. Thank God for that!

Salvation Brings Joy and Peace

All of this wonderful truth may be followed up by calling attention to the glorious blessings that flow from a salvation which is full and free. Everyone, I believe, longs deep down within for a settled peace and calm assurance. That is what we may have merely by believing—truly believing, or exercising faith.

Romans 15:13 says, "Now may the God of hope fill you with all joy and peace in believing, that ye may abound in hope." Observe that it is just by "believing" that we may have both joy and peace and hope. In First Peter it is put this way, "Though you do not see him, yet believing, you exult with a joy unspeakable and triumphant" (I Peter 1:8). The blessed results that can come from believing are referred to when it is said, "We then who have believed shall enter into his rest" (Hebrews 4:3). Why make these blessings more difficult than God makes them? First John 3:19 says, "We know that we are of the truth, and in his sight we set our hearts at rest." Thank God for His glorious rest!

Jude speaks of "Him who is able to preserve you . . . without blemish in gladness" (Verse 24), while in Colossians we read, "He has reconciled you . . . to present you holy and undefiled and irreproachable before him" (1:22). What have we to fear then? The promises of God are sure and unfailing toward us. We may say the past is *completely pardoned,* the present is *abundantly provided* for, the future is *faithfully promised.* What a bountiful God we have!

Many would-be Christians lack that repose which comes from faith, perhaps never having realized that it is possible. It is simply a matter of taking God at His word. We first believe what He has said about our redemption being already accomplished and being complete, and then believe these promises about keeping us and bestowing His peace upon us. Philippians 4:6, 7, says, "Have no anxiety. . . . And may the peace of God which surpasses all understanding guard your hearts and your minds in Christ Jesus."

Some may think that their sin and unworthiness have placed them beyond the scope of this peace. But in Luke 7 we read of one "who was a sinner" (Verse 37), who, nevertheless, upon coming to Jesus in humble sincerity, was given His gracious word, "Thy faith hath saved thee; go in peace" (Verse 50). Therefore it certainly is possible for any of us.

The eighth chapter of Romans puts it this way: "There is therefore now no condemnation for those who are in Christ Jesus. . . . Now you have not received a spirit of bondage so as to be again in fear, but you have received a spirit of adoption as sons . . . we are sons of God. . . . If God be for us, who is against us? . . .Who shall separate us from the love of Christ? . . . In all these things we overcome because of him who has loved us. For I am sure that neither death, nor life, nor angels, nor principalities, nor things present, nor things to come, nor powers, nor height, nor depth, nor any other creature will be able to separate us from the love of God, which is in Christ Jesus our Lord" (Verses 1, 15, 16, 31, 35, 37-39).

84

Returning to the fact of believing being the key to all this, we see it forcibly put in the Gospel of John. The words "believe," "believing," and "believeth" occur over one hundred times in those twenty-one chapters. In fact, the book was given by the Spirit of God for this very reason: "These are written that you may believe that Jesus is the Christ, the Son of God, and that believing you may have life in his name" (20:31). Over and over again salvation or eternal life is said to depend upon believing. Read the book and see how it stands out. Then observe the further blessings of security and assurance which come from believing.

"Jesus said, 'He who comes to me shall not hunger, and he who believes in me shall never thirst. . . . Him who comes to me I will not cast out'" (6:35, 37).

"'If therefore the Son makes you free, you will be free indeed'" (8:36).

"'I am the door. If anyone enter by me he shall be safe. . . . I came that they may have life, and have it more abundantly'" (10:9, 10).

"'I have come a light into the world, that whoever believes in me may not remain in the darkness'" (12:46).

The Simplicity of True Belief

But here it may be asked, *what does it mean to believe in Christ?* And, you may say, *I thought I always believed in Christ.* Most, of us, to be sure, have believed much about Christ. That is, we have believed historical facts about Him. But that is not taking His actual word by faith. Sin came upon the human race through disbelief in God's word (Genesis 3); salvation comes to members of the human race by believing God's word.

To truly believe is to fully accept by faith what God has said: what He has said about our sin and need, what He has said about His paying the full price of our sins, what He has said about freely forgiving those who put their trust in Him—and then leaving the matter there as settled. It is believing God with all our heart (Proverbs 3:5; Romans 10:9), and receiving Christ as Savior into our heart (Ephesians 3:17; I Peter 3:15; Apocalypse 3:20).

True belief is not merely a passive assent to some creed or dogma, but an active embracing of the divine provision made for man in Christ. We accept historical facts in our minds; we receive a divine Person in our hearts. To bring this out, we find in John 1:12 that "believe" and "receive" are used as synonyms, or interchangeably; that is, to "believe" on Him is to "receive" Him, with the result of becoming a child of God. "To as many as *received* him he gave the power of becoming sons of God, to those who *believe* in his name."

True belief or faith is trust in and reliance on an object. In the realm of the soul, it is trust in and reliance on Christ alone as Savior. It is complete confidence *in* and dependence *on* Him. Therefore, as one trusts and relies on Christ he gives up all of his own efforts, otherwise he is not relying wholly on Christ. If we rely *entirely* on Christ, we do not rely on our own works.

To help us understand this, the word which in our Bibles is over and over again rendered "believe" is sometimes translated "commit to," or "trust" one's self to. That is what real belief is. The word is translated (in the Confraternity version) "committed to" (Galatians 2:7; I Timothy 1:11; Titus 1:3), and it appears as "entrust" or "entrusted" (Luke 16:11; Romans 3:2; I Corinthians 9:17; I Thessalonians 2:4), and as "trust" himself to (John 2:24).

Just as when a child's father says, "Jump and I will catch you," and the child believes and acts upon it, so by faith the believer lets go of everything else and drops into the eternal arms of the omnipotent Savior. That is just what true faith or belief is: *trusting one's self to the Savior by committing the soul's salvation to Him.* Then, if one fully commits himself to Christ for his salvation, it means that he is not trusting in his own efforts or good works, nor in churchly functions and sacraments, to achieve the selfsame thing.

Note that it is the **object** of faith—**Christ**—that saves, not faith itself. Faith is merely the agency or instrument, though a very necessary one. But do not look at your faith; *look to Christ!* That is, do not look inwardly (introspection), but look outwardly, or up to Christ. It might even be said: little or weak faith in a strong object (Christ) is far better than much faith in a weak object (one's own doings). So again let it be said, **the value of faith lies not in itself but in the value of its Object.**

Any normal human being can exercise that faith if he will (John 5:40; 7:17, 37). Of course, he must first recognize the Object of that faith—the Savior who died for him and who promises to cleanse him from all his sins. Recognizing that, he then must take God's word for it, and that is all—that is faith.

Having come to see what real faith is which God asks of each of us, why not bow your head right where you are and earnestly ask the Lord Jesus to forgive you of all your sins and tell Him that you are now receiving Him as your only Savior and Lord? Make it a very personal thing. Repeat it until you can say, "I live in the faith of the Son of God, who loved *me* and gave himself up for *me*" (Galatians 2:20). Then rejoice as you find that Christ's finished work makes you safe, His keeping power makes you secure, His faithful word makes you sure.

Having done this you may be assured of God's presence and help to you personally. The Lord has said to us, "Him who comes to me I will not cast out" (John 6:37); and "He himself has said, 'I will not leave thee, neither will I forsake thee.' So that we may confidently say, 'The Lord is my helper: I will not fear what man shall do to me'" (Hebrews 13:5, 6).

I may conclude this part by calling attention to three promises of the Lord Jesus, one each in the fourteenth, fifteenth and sixteenth chapters of John's Gospel (in His upper room discourse). He says to those who have become His own by faith, "Peace I leave with you, my peace I give to you; not as the world gives do I give to you. Do not let your heart be troubled, or be afraid." "These things I have spoken to you that my joy may be in you, and that your joy may be made full." "In me you may have peace. In the world you will have affliction. But take courage, I have overcome the world" (John 14:27; 15:11; 16:33).

Don't you long to know all this? Believe it, and it is yours!

*　　*　　*　　*　　*

Teresa, I have gone about as far as we need to go. There are a number of other subjects which we could discuss, but we have considered the leading ones. If you want to weigh things further, I could only suggest that you again go over what we have taken up. If that is not enough, I don't think anything else would be. Maybe what I have set forth seems to leave only spot pictures, but if you go back over them I think you will now see how they all fit together and form a comprehensive train of thought.

I trust, Teresa, you understand that I have been writing to you as a true friend. I only want to help you. If all of this were something of minor significance I would let it go. I would not consider it worth the effort if it all didn't matter much one way or the other. But it is of tremendous importance: *a soul's eternal destiny depends upon his being in right relation to God.*

Believe me, I hate to see a good friend get entangled in a system which falls short of what is God's very best for us. The church which you are interested in may be very thorough in religious practices; it has great appeal to the esthetic sense; it supplies something which seems to meet man's basic religious instincts; it even passes under the great name of Christianity, which gives it high respectability. But, remember, it is not respectable "religion" which man needs, but the regenerating power of the gospel in the soul. We need full assurance of forgiveness of all sins now, and the certainty of eternal life through union with Christ. And that is just what God has freely provided and wants us to take directly from Him.

I believe you can see that I am not pleading for "Protestantism," as such. We readily admit its failures in many areas. Many so-called Protestants are weak in faith, careless in their conduct and half-hearted in living up to what they profess to know. They themselves need to have a fresh vision of the mighty redemption wrought by Christ and of the infinite grace of God toward sinners. They need to take more seriously the Bible and the fullness of the blessed truths revealed therein. Thy need to turn their eyes more fully upon the Lord and His readiness to work in the lives of His people, and they should not be so occupied with secondary things.

On the other side of the ledger, Catholics possess many admirable characteristics. Many of them display commendable sincerity. Numbers of them have exemplified a worthy spirit of sacrifice. They demonstrate much that shows their concern in the field of charity. But all of this means little if the heart of God's truth is overshadowed by external things.

The supreme need is that Protestants and Catholics alike should go back to the Holy Bible and search the sacred pages, determining to bring everything into conformity with its plain teachings.

As you have observed, I have made my basic appeal to the

87

inspired Word of God. There should be no argument here. We must either take God's Word for things, or we are rejecting the clear testimony of Holy Scripture. I have concentrated only on truths which are unquestionably revealed within its sacred pages. I have quoted over and over again from what it sets forth. You have a copy of it. But have you been reading it? Take it at its face value. Let it speak directly to your heart and soul.

You have had the truth of God placed before you. Now you will have to make your own decision as to which way you are going. Other points that might be raised are minor. When I say you will have to choose, that seems rather cold—like a take-it-or-leave-it proposition. But, believe me, I do not say it lightly or with indifference, as though it means little to me. Beyond anything I can say, I hate to see a single soul turn in the wrong direction. Too much is in the balance. Eternal issues are involved.

If a person goes on and identifies himself with a set of teachings to which, in his inner heart and conscience, he cannot give wholehearted assent, he then becomes a hypocrite. If he gives outward acquiescence to that which he has reason to doubt is really the full truth of God, and if he continues therein, he is acting a lie. Let us be honest with our own souls. We dare not trifle with our unending destiny. Turn to Christ in His fullness and let Him free you from all trammels. His personal promise is, *"You shall know the truth, and the truth shall make you free. . . . If therefore the Son makes you free, you will be free indeed"* (John 8:32, 36).

Decision for Christ

You have read the beautiful story of salvation's simplicity in Christ, discovering many plain Scriptures stating that redemption is received by grace alone through faith. Now will you trust Him for the salvation He has already provided through His death, burial and resurrection? If so, indicate it by signing the following decision form. Then, as soon as possible, let others know of the stand you have taken.

Biblical Evangelism Press
P. O. Box 157
Brownsburg, Indiana 46112

Gentlemen:

I confess that I am a sinner deserving the eternal judgment of God in Hell forever because of my wickedness. But I also believe that Jesus Christ made possible my salvation through His atoning work on the cross. Right now, as honestly as I know how, I repent of my sins and ask Him to save me. I do now open my heart to the Lord Jesus Christ and invite Him in. I trust Him to give me everlasting life now and take me to Heaven when I die, just as He promised.

I will not trust in any church to save me, nor in any religious ritual. I now trust

Jesus Christ and Him alone. As soon as I have opportunity, I will confess Him before others as my Lord and Savior. With His help, I want to live for Him the rest of my life.

(Signed) ---

Address ---

City ------------------------------- State ---------- Zip ----------

If you will copy the above or write us in your own words, we will send you a letter of counsel and encouragement. Now that you have honestly received Christ into your heart, you should be baptized and unite with a Bible-believing church.

BIBLIOGRAPHY

Works Quoted in This Book

Addis, William E., and Arnold, Thomas. *A Catholic Dictionary*. Revised by Scannell, T. B., Hallett, P. E., Albion, G., Seventeenth Edition. London: Routledge & Kegan Paul Ltd., 1960.

Arendzen, J. P. *The New Testament*, According to the Douay Version, with Introduction and Notes. London: Sheed & Ward, 1947.

Attwater, Donald. *A Catholic Dictionary*, (The Catholic Encyclopaedic Dictionary), Second Edition, Revised. New York: The Macmillan Co., 1949.

Baltimore Catechism. See herein: Deck, E.M.; Kinkead, T.L.; compare also, Spirago, F.

Bible, Holy, The. *The Holy Bible*, Translated from the Latin Vulgate,. . .Containing Bishop Challoner's Notes. London: Burns, Oates & Washbourne Ltd. Preface, Cardinal Bourne, Archbishop of Westminster, 1914. See also herein: Arendzen; New Testament; New American Bible.

Catechism Of The Council of Trent. Issued by order of Pope Pius V. Translated by McHugh, J. A., and Callan, C. J. New York: Joseph F. Wagner, Inc., Ninth Printing, 1945.

Deck, E. M. *The Baltimore Catechism, No. 3,* With Explanations. Eighth Edition. Buffalo, New York: Rauch & Stoeckl Printing Co., 1933.

Forrest, M. D. *Who Is The Pope?* New York: The Paulist Press, 1931.

Geiermann, P. *A Manual Of Theology For The Laity*. New, Revised Edition, New York: Benziger Brothers, 1906.

Gibbons, James Cardinal. *The Faith Of Our Fathers*. One Hundred and Tenth Revised Edition. New York: P. J. Kenedy & Sons, n.d.

Hartman, L. F. See below: *New American Bible, The.*

Herzog, Charles G., S. J. *Channels Of Redemption*. New York: Benziger Brothers, 1931.

Hugel, F. Von. See below: Von Hugel.

Kinkead, Thomas L. *An Explanation Of The Baltimore Catechism of Christian Doctrine*. New York: Benziger Brothers, 1921.

New American Bible, The. Translated by members of the Catholic Biblical Association of America, Sponsored by the Bishop's Committee of the Confraternity of Christian Doctrine, Louis F. Hartman, Editor in Chief. New York: Benziger, Inc., 1970.

New Testament, The. A Revision of the Challoner-Rheims Version, Edited by Catholic Scholars under the Patronage of the Episcopal Committee of the Confraternity of Christian Doctrine. Paterson, New Jersey: St. Anthony Guild Press, 1941.

Nichols, J. B. *Evangelical Belief*. London: The Religious Tract Society, 1903.

O'Brien, John A. *The Faith of Millions*. Ninth Edition, Revised. Huntington, Indiana, Our Sunday Visitor, 1938.

Rome and The Study of Scripture. A Collection of Papal Enactments. . .with the Decisions of the Biblical Commission. Sixth Edition, Revised & Enlarged. St. Meinrad, Indiana, Grail Publications, 1958.

Sixteen Documents of Vatican II. N.C.W.C. Translation. Boston, Massachusetts, Daughters of St. Paul, n.d.

Spirago, Francis, and Clarke, R. F. *The Catechism Explained*, An Exhaustive Exposition. . .New York: Benziger Brothers, 1927.

Trese, Leo J. *The Faith Explained*. Notre Dame, Indiana: Fides Publishers Assn., 1959.

Valensin, A., and Huby, J. *The Word of Salvation*, Translation and Explanation of the Gospel according to St. Luke. Translated by J. J. Heenan. Milwaukee: The Bruce Publishing Co., 1957.

Vatican II, Decrees of. See above: *Sixteen Documents of Vatican II*.

Von Hugel, Baron Friedrich. *Some Notes On The Petrine Claims*. London: Sheed & Ward, 1930.

Wilmers, W. and Conway, J. *Handbook Of The Christian Religion*. Revised according to the New Code of Canon Law. Second Edition. New York: Benziger Brothers, 1921.

Yorke, P. C. *The Mass*. Third Edition. San Francisco: The Text Book Publishing Co., 1926.

Richard Thomas. An anthology of The Columbia Catalogue of Christian Serials. New York: The Macmillan, 1951.

New American Bible. Sponsored by members of the Catholic Biblical Association of America. Sponsored by members of the Catholic Bishops' Committee of the Confraternity of Christian Doctrine. Camden, New York: Thomas Nelson Publishers, 1971.

New Testament. The New Translation of the Catholic Biblical Version. Edited by Catholic Scholars under the patronage of the Episcopal Committee of the Confraternity of Christian Doctrine. Paterson, New Jersey: St. Anthony Guild Press, 1941.

Nicholas, J. B. Henri Holt (Ed.) Essay. London: The Johns Ltd Publications, 1965.

Other Bible. The Torah Multilevel. 3rd Edition. Revised. Huntington, Indiana: Our Sunday Visitor, 1973.

Romaine, The Changeless Word. A Collection of Basic Statements, With the permission of the Biblical Confraternity Bible. Edited. Lanked & Engineered, St. Marysd, Indiana. Guild Publications 1956.

Seven Centuries of the Christ. By W. C. Translation. Boston: Blue Edition Commission. 1966. Four Tom.

Seregio, Landa. Ann Arbor: The Michigan Press.

Sequoyer, An Illustrated Exposition. New York: Doubleday Brothers, 1966.

Traus, Jacob. The Virgin Represented Notre Dame, Indiana Bible Publisher's Association, 1967.

Edition, J. J. and Helen J. The Works of Translation and Explanation of The Gospel according to St. Luke. Translated by J. C. London: The Unlimited, The Press Publishing Co. 1966.

Wolfson, H. Doctrines of the above of Christian Documents, Cambridge.

Vine, Flügel, Hebrew Hebrew the Gospels according Revised Edition. London: Oxford Ann, 1966.

Summer, W. and Black, A. E. Dictionaries of the Christian Religion. Revised paperback. The Gospel of Deacon Luke. Second edition. New York: Benziger Brothers, 1962.

Wine, W. G. Vine. Third Edition, New Explained, The Text Book. Philadelphia, 1959.